Prostate Cancer is (not) Funny

The True Story of a Smartass and His Prostate

Dan Lasz

Illustrations by Zeana Boy

Prostate Cancer is (not) Funny

Copyright © 2012 by Dan Laszlo

www.prostatecancerisnotfunny.com

First Edition

Illustrations by Zeana Bey

Interior graphics by Dan Laszlo

Cover design by Mark Bloch (www.panmodern.com)

ISBN-10: 0615695523

ISBN-13: 978-0615695525

DEDICATION

For Leah, for your love, patience, humor, support, and encouragement. If I could make one wish for my prostate-challenged peers, well, actually it would be that sex cured prostate cancer. But if I could make a second wish, it would be that all men had a partner like Leah to accompany them along their painful paths, for I know that the challenges I faced, and continue to face, are immeasurably eased because I take them on them with Leah at my side.

And for Sam, for understanding sarcasm at an early age, for being patient during my recovery when playtime wasn't always as fun as he wished, and for never making fun of Dad in his diaper.

CONTENTS

ACKNOWLEDGMENTS

Many men die from or are severely affected by prostate cancer and I realize that prostate cancer is not funny for these men, their friends, or families. My thoughts are with my prostate-challenged peers who did not, or will not survive this disease and I stand with those whose quality of life is severely diminished. I ask the reader's indulgence in responding to the common challenges we face with levity, sarcasm, impudence, and at times, irreverence and vulgarity.

I am grateful to my primary care physician for detecting my problem early enough to successfully treat it and to the doctors and nurses at the University of California, San Francisco Medical Center for their professionalism and humanity. I'm grateful enough to maintain all my medical care providers' anonymity.

Special thanks to Zeana Bey for her dedication to bringing my vision to life in her inspired and bawdy illustrations. I know that it was sometimes awkward to draw prostates and penises in Starbucks but that didn't stop her.

Thanks to Mark Bloch for the fun and artful cover design.

Love and gratitude to my wife Leah for her unattributed contributions to the content, for reading and editing the many iterations, and for pushing me to finish this therapeutic work.

The honesty in my writing—no matter how embarrassing or self-incriminating—would not have been possible without the example set by Howard Stern. The truth will set you free.

CHAPTER 1

TO PEE OR NOT TO PEE, THAT IS THE PROBLEM

In 2008 my prostate and I were separated due to irreconcilable differences—I wanted to live and it wanted to metastasize.

Prostate cancer is not funny, but if you'd rather laugh than cry about it, you're in the right book.

This bad joke begins differently for each man. Maybe you're tired of getting up in the middle of the night to pee. Or maybe you have a slowing stream, which is a kind way to say that you ain't pissin' like a racehorse anymore. All your life you have walked into the little boys room, unzipped and taken a nice pee—aaaaaaaaaahhhhh! On a warm summer day if the potty feng shui was just right, it sounded like a waterfall in there—you took a serene, happy pee. Full stream ahead, you backed away from the urinal, carefully monitoring your forceful arc—you might have been mistaken for a marble baroque fountain, except you didn't have the benefit of a marble penis for accuracy—sometimes it got messy in there.

Remember how much fun it was to target that little blue deodorizer in the urinal? Your mission? Hit dead center on that flowering oasis blooming in the stench of a stark white desert. Your stream struck that little blue devil with the dead-on precision of a modern day smart bomb targeting an enemy's weapons armory.

It's not the same hitting the head in your fifties: Maybe you have stood over a urinal, like some poor schmuck, and pleaded with your penis to perform. But instead of a single smart bomb streaming precisely into the center of its target, your attack appears more like a dozen fat scatter bombs exploding randomly with the precision of, well, the precision of a 50 year old pressure-challenged penis.

It might not be that bad, but as your forty's recede with your hairline, your pissin' starts to be more ebb and less flow. It may have sounded like a waterfall during the innocent pees of your teens, but now, it's easier to imagine a clock ticking away—tick, tock—drip, drop. And that clock is marking the passage of youth for those of us stuck in puer aeternus—a condition better known as the Peter Pan Syndrome, which arises from an inability to come to terms with aging.

When my penis began to drip urine like a dysfunctional faucet my psyche began a mid-life transformation. In the mystic light of the bathroom I turned inward—my mind's eye imagined the radiant long haired youth of my teens. However, the cruel mirror of reality reflected an over-ripe hippie. A short period of cognitive dissonance was followed by a rude awakening—that old man in the mirror can't piss and neither can I. Hey, that old man is me!

Now I know why I am invisible to the 20-something beauties that Sean Connery and I used to attract (and he still does). Had I inadvertently become one of those men my daughters call creepy? Were the pretty women I smiled at pretty revolted?

I attended my 30th high school reunion some years ago. So many in my cohort had aged badly—balding, jowly, thick in the middle. Now it was undeniable—so had I. I guess I have come to terms with aging. That is supposed to be a good thing, right? Then why did it feel so....so...bad?

And so, you may find yourself in front of the urinal with the ache of real urgency, but your urine hesitates to board the train departing from Track No. 1. The cold, cruel urinal, with its passage down the silver drain into the great unknown, is just too much for your prostate to bear.

"NO!" your prostate screams boldly from beneath your bladder.

"You can't make me!" it cries like a four year old.

But whereas four year olds don't make the rules, your prostate is Lord of the Pee. You can rant and you can rave but you just can't make your prostate behave—it bows to a greater master.

OK, get this symptom of prostate cancer—burning urination. How would you like to piss fire? That is a superpower you would find difficult to use, my friend. You will not become a member of the Fantastic Four with the ability to shoot fire from your penis. They will not expand to five for FirePecker.

What's the upside of a burning penis?

Lighting the family barbecue is inappropriate.

And just try to appear suave lighting a cigarette in health conscious California. It's nearly impossible to look dignified lighting up a smoke in public in the Golden State, especially when lighting up with your penis.

And the class of woman that is impressed with a cock light may be the kind of girl you can take home, but not the kind of girl you can take home to mom.

Great balls of fire! Go ahead and ask her!

Mom: "So, how did you two meet?"

Smok'n hot babe: "Oh, Dick did the cutest thing! I was fumbling for a match when he just whips his cock out, right there at the end of the bar, and lights my butt from like four feet away. He totally burned the competition. He literally burned *one* of them. Anyway, I was so impressed with your little Dick."

Mom: "Richard, a moment please?"

The symptoms go from bad to worse. Pray you don't have a painful ejaculation. A painful orgasm? That can't be—that's an oxymoron! But check it out at prostatecancerfoundation.org. It *is* a symptom of prostate cancer. That tells you how funny-and cruel prostate cancer is—what other disease could give you a painful orgasm? But that explains the position of the prostate—it's between your rectum and your penis—between heaven and hell—between exit and enter—between stink and shrink—between a rectum and a used-to-get-harder place.

These are the more civilized symptoms of a problematic prostate. How would you like to find blood in your urine or semen? Blood in your semen? If the woman in your life finds semen distasteful under the best of circumstances wait until she reacts to bloody semen! Do you think she will believe you when you tell her you delivered red sperm for Valentine's Day? "How romantic." She'll coo as she rolls over, and grabs the remote. She'll turn on the news as quickly as you turned her off.

Maybe you've had a digital rectal exam—a particularly cruel probe. The doctor inserts a gloved (you hope) finger into your behind to feel the prostate through the wall of your rectum. A tumor in the prostate can sometimes be detected as a hard lump.

Maybe you were laying there, so pathetic, so miserable, with a doctor's finger up your bum. With a slip of the tongue the doctor mutters, "Uh, oh. That doesn't feel good."

"You're damn right that doesn't feel good!" you respond automatically. Then you think "Uh oh? What do you mean, uh oh?"

A prostate's problems are revealed in myriad ways, and sometimes, very subtly. I didn't really have any of these symptoms. Let me tell you what happened to me.

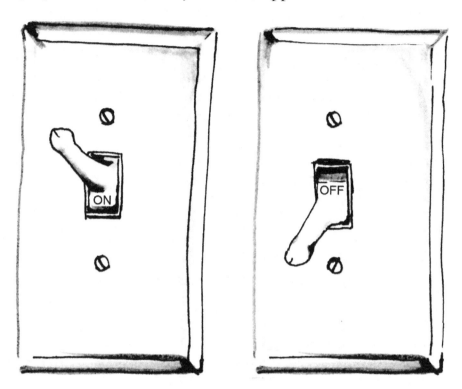

In 2007 my libido switched off

It felt like its switch just flipped from "on" to "off." If you have never been switched-on—obsessed with sex, always on the prowl, putting out the signals, playing the games, seducing, and being generally deceitful in order to get women into bed—the only way to understand the state of "on" is to view it as the same irrational and uncontrollable behavior of an addict feeding his addiction. It makes a good man bad. The Torah says that God hears the tears of women. That isn't good news for men who are switched-on.

And if you have never been switched-off—not just indifferent to, but completely uninterested in sex—I can't tell you how strange "off" is. Not needing sex, not wanting sex. It was not normal. And it was normal. I can tell you one difference between switched-on and switched-off. I was occasionally ashamed of my actions when I was switched-on. I was always ashamed of my inactions when I was switched-off. Actively causing tears in women you did not love for your unbridled drive for sex does not compare to passively causing tears in the woman you do love for not desiring her sexually. It takes two to have a great sexual relationship but only one is needed for symbiotic neutering.

A low libido was definitely not normal for me. I have been sexually oriented most of my life. From 1974 to 1995, I was a perpetual college student in no small part because of the freshmen women that debuted every fall. If you are young, immature, love women, and live in a college town you bear summer break like Gollum bore his empty ring finger— Where is my precious? Even Gollum might have forgotten The One Ring for The Many Women that arrived each fall term.

As a graduate student in the 1980s, I held a nice place in the academic hierarchy—I taught, and yet I was a student. As a teaching assistant in the Mathematics Department I was in exactly the right place in the pecking order—above undergraduates and below professors. As an undergraduate, you are one among the throng of horny, pimply faced dorm kids. As a professor, you are considered a lech for ogling your students—worse for dating one. As a graduate student you are mysterious, sophisticated, supposedly intelligent, experienced, and know your way around town. So yes, I was a perpetual student—and perpetually dating.

I have matured and evolved from that sophomoric state of mind and have been blessed with a long and happy marriage.

And as 2006—the year Dick Cheney would shoot his friend in a hunting accident—transitioned to 2007—the year Apple introduced the IPhone--my wife Leah's sex drive outpaced my own.

Leah in Graceland on Elvis' Bed

Sadly, in 2007 Elvis' bed was getting more action than my bed—and Elvis was dead!

I was, and am still very attracted to Leah. If I hadn't made her image somewhat anonymous to protect her dignity (oh, the embarrassing details that are to come) you would see that she is much more beautiful than a schlub like me deserves.

Leah's Graceland prayers didn't seem to work.

We didn't need the plastic protection on Elvis' bed, or any other kind of protection. That's my side on the right—with the "PLEASE DO NOT TOUCH" sign.

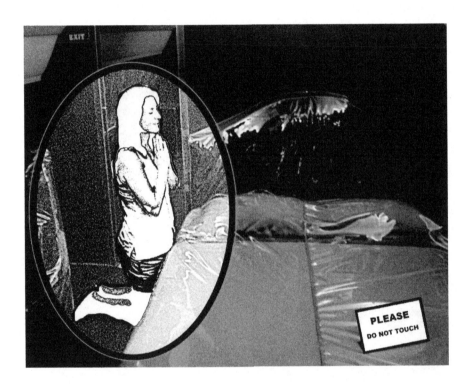

The Real Desperate Housewife
of Central California

Leah became desperate when I preferred watching Desperate Housewives to having sex, when Sex in the City became foreplay to sleep, and when I began to read Playboy just for the articles. God heard more than Leah's tears. God heard her prayers.

The decline in my libido seemed unnatural. This was not normal. You get the idea—in 2007 I wasn't myself.

OK, maybe I couldn't be this guy anymore…

…but I know I could still be this guy!

Leah wondered if my testosterone was on the wane. It was possible. Testosterone declines with age and we've already determined that I was aging.

I didn't see a home testosterone test kit at the drugstore so I visited my Primary Care Physician—Dr. PCP. I was determined to get my manhood back.

Spoiler alert: By the end of this book I do get manhood back. But it is not *my* manhood. Whoever's manhood I got wasn't as good as mine.

I got someone else's shitty manhood.

Dan Laszlo

CHAPTER 2

THE PROBE: BOLDLY GOING WHERE NO MAN HAS GONE BEFORE

I should have known that there would be a probe waiting for me at Dr. PCP's office. Doctors love to probe. An odd breed of treasure hunter, doctors eagerly dig through layers of human cells in pursuit of anomalous artifacts. They probe our bodily cavities with wood, metal, and electronic instruments in search of physical or biological signs of distress.

Doctors probe gleefully. This probably starts in their youth. I imagine they loved getting dirty as little kids by digging in the sand, the yard, mud puddles, or any opening they could get their little hands into.

The intensity and inappropriateness of a physician's probing increases over the years. The Probe begins innocently in one's childhood at the pediatrician's office with the wielding of a flat, wide popsicle stick and the rally "Open your mouth wide and say ahhhhh!" But they had already eaten the popsicle. What was the point?

Harmless enough—probe on! It's not a threat when Curious Doc jams his pointy Otoscope into your ear in pursuit of, what? Waxy buildup? It only becomes a threat when you are assaulted with a shot in the arm. A shot is not like those gentler probes. Those probes were only reconnaissance missions to gather a little *intel*. Enter an *existing* orifice and look, maybe touch, but that's it. In—out—take a lollipop. Open wide—say ahh—in—out—take a lollipop. A peek in the ear—in—out—take a lollipop.

A shot represents a sea-change with respect to the patient-physician relationship. In—*deposit some mysterious fluid*—out—cry like a little girl—and, bite me, screw the lollipop. What the hell? Do you *have to* punch a new hole in my body with a needle? You have the ears, nostrils, mouth, butt and genitals and that isn't enough? True, I'd rather have a new entrance drilled than utilize the butt or genitals. Nothing but you and your soul mate should have access to those parts.

Innocence lost—the shot feels wrong to a kid. It is wrong. It is the first indication that the physician is not just a big friend. And we are clueless about the multitude of tricks in our doctor's repertoire—the cold sterile tools—the blood tests—the disposable gloves.

When a male hits the teen years the strange-factor is ratcheted up. Drop your pants, turn your head, and cough? That probe is inappropriate at best. "Hey! Those are my balls you're squeezing!" The dispassionate testicle fondle is a new twist—a mysterious and very friendly probe to detect a hernia.

But have you ever seen anyone with a hernia? A hernia is painful. Why the hell do you need a scrotum massage to detect it? Isn't the screaming clue enough? Turn your head and cough, indeed. Your doctor gives you an order and you comply—the doctor is the authority. If your doctor told you to shut your eyes tightly and holler—a blink and a shout— you would do it. And so we accept a gentle touch to our balls. We do turn our heads. We do cough. Why? Because the doctor asked us to.

It's as if the doctor is a Jedi master practicing his Jedi mind control. And so, when Dr. Yoda waves his hand in front of your face and says…

Bend over you will.

…you bend over. Jedi mind control, *my ass*.

The Penultimate Probe: The digital rectal exam. The hernia check is only a modest prelude to the humiliation of the infinitely more invasive probe known as the DRE—digital rectal exam. If you are relatively young, technically savvy, and facing your first digital rectal exam you might smile, thinking you are about to sit your ass down on your IPhone. There's an app for that, right?. Think again, newbie—this *is* your father's digital rectal exam.

Nothing prepares a man for a lubricated latex-covered finger up the bum. We may protest, but give a someone a title like "Doctor" and we submit. It seems like just about everything has traveled to the forbidden zone by the time you hit your fifties.

And what goes up the bum comes out—you can't really lose anything up there. I guess you can store it for a while, but you can't lose it, can you? I only cried once after a doctor's rectal expedition, but I have to admit, it was a good cry.

Men wince when Doc Ock puts on the latex and some lube.

But hold the phone! What the hell is a doctor's finger doing up my butt in the 21st century?

Seriously, get your damn finger out of my ass, doc. A transportation security agent with a little training can detect a vial of hotel shampoo buried in my carry-on at airport security with a glance at a monitor.

You would think that a doctor, with a bazillion years of education and with a full arsenal of state-of-the-art technology could detect a problematic prostate without having to stick a finger up your ass.

You would think. But no, there you are lying on an examining table, in the fetal position, feeling far too intimate with Dr. PCP.

The Digital Rectal Exam

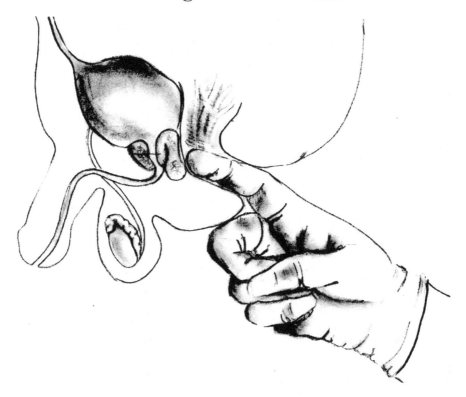

It's not polite to point, Doc!

And you hear his chipper voice: "Everything feels normal!"

Like hell that feels normal! It is a violation. A bowel moving violation. As I said, little kids like to get dirty and doctors like to probe. I guess little kids who grow up with puer aeternus—peter pan syndrome—but manage to become doctors like to get dirty when they probe. Viva la proctologist.

If there was any thought to good marketing in the medical profession they would figure out a way to make you feel manly during the DRE. That seems like a tough nut to crack. But, perhaps something like…

Market research indicates that if you can get the customer in the door your finger is already halfway up his butt. The medical world would benefit from more smart marketing like the Jenna-DRE table. It's not like hospitals don't have a lot in common with all-inclusive resorts. Maybe they should start with a catchy name…like, uh, Club Med?

And Club Med is gender-agnostic—an equal opportunity humiliator. Why stop at making men cringe?

When a woman hears *"place your feet in the stirrups,"* she can only hope she is about to mount a stallion.

But hold the phone…

Don't you think the gynecological experience would be enhanced if a women was told to *"place your feet in these lovely red pumps?"* My wife would eagerly anticipate her next visit—maybe something in a black patent leather stiletto.

I know, I might be a smartass but I am also a marketing genius.

God works in mysterious ways. Medical invasions on our dignity give rise to thoughts about how we would do things differently. But how presumptuous are we for thinking that the mosquito was a mistake or that God could have provided a more civilized route to the prostate?

Apparently we are still paying the price for eating from The Tree of Knowledge. Had we never known modesty, we might be more comfortable having our balls fondled by Dr. PCP during the hernia check, or having his latex gloved finger up our booties during a DRE.

So basically Eve screwed us all.

And it doesn't seem like it was even a great apple.

I don't recall Eve saying "Mmmmm, that is such a good apple! You have to taste this, Adam."

Nope. She went straight from the bite to "Adam, are my boobs too small? Why don't you ever dress for dinner? Oh wow, your balls are gross." And that's when God gets pissed off.

"WHAT DO YOU MEAN BALLS ARE GROSS? WHAT PART OF CREATED IN MY IMAGE DO YOU NOT GET?"

Complain that mosquitoes are God's mistake, no problem— God gets that all the time. But complain about the scrotum and you start to press God's buttons.

Most people think it was eating of The Tree that got us kicked out of the garden. Nope. It was the balls bashing. Perhaps if there had been a wider variety of magic trees. The Tree of Sensitivity, perhaps. Eve might have said "You know Adam, this fig leaf is just so *you*." We'd still be in the Garden of Eden. Prostate cancer doesn't grow there.

This means war. We can place these bodily probes in the context of war. We prepare for war against disease from the moment of our birth. Our pediatrician led the charge in our youth. He began with regularly scheduled reconnaissance missions into our bodies through conventional access points. Existing routes like the ear, nose, or mouth required only a passport to enter. Once inside he gathered intelligence on potential enemy actions against our biological systems.

Reconnaissance missions were limited to looking and touching—no direct engagement with the enemy was authorized. Open wide. Say ah. Eventually it got dirty—war is hell. Bend over. Say ow.

A military option is always on the table. Our strategy includes deploying troops to engage the enemy on our own soil. Kids experience the shot before they can talk. It is a covert operation—conventional passage through open ports won't do. We show no passport—we force a point of entry. A route through the arm is our first choice but a shot in the booty is a classic military tactic.

Troops injected in your body may carry a vaccine as a preventative action—we are stationing troops as a deterrent. On the other hand, injected steroids go to battle—they seek and destroy the insurgency led by poison oak. In a full blown war, chemotherapy advances throughout the body in a chemical march as an aggressive response to enemy cancer. Technologically enhanced military actions of this form include radiation therapy—lasers shoot photons—elementary particles—through the skin into the war zone to take out the DNA of cancer cells so they stop reproducing.

The final form of battle is extraction—Special Ops Forces enter and remove the enemy or key informants from the body. The most extreme form of extraction includes the removal of an inflamed appendix or the prostate. The least extreme form of extraction is a swab taken from the mouth. Somewhere in between lies the biopsy.

And that brings us back to my story.

Remember, I thought I might have low testosterone. Dr. PCP agreed that it was worth checking out. A blood test proved us right—my testosterone was very low. That explained my fascination with Desperate Housewives and my bond with Oprah.

Men's testosterone levels typically peak in their late teens or early twenties and begin a gradual decline in their thirties.

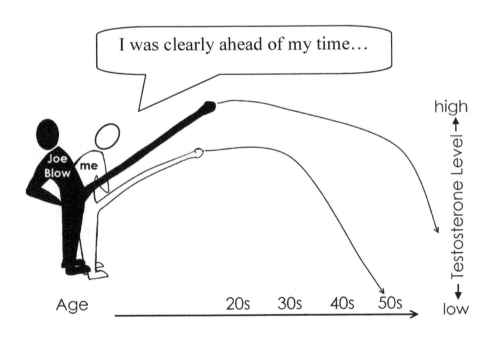

We discussed options for testosterone treatments. However, before we could begin we had to be certain I did not have prostate cancer. Because, as it turns out, testosterone feeds prostate cancer like gas fuels a fire.

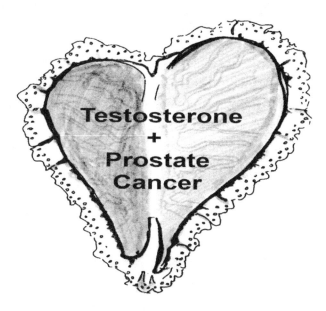

And so, my physician prescribed my first PSA test. PSA stands for Pubic Service Announcement—it announces potential prostate problems—cancer or benign prostate enlargement, for example.

A PSA test might be ordered in response to one or more of the drippy symptoms I described in Chapter 1, or even in celebration of hitting your fifties. Prostate Specific Antigen, which coincidentally also has PSA as its monogram, is a protein produced by the cells of the prostate gland. When all is well, little or no PSA is present in the bloodstream. It all stays in the greedy prostate, where it does the job it was meant to do—liquefy semen so that sperm can swim freely. But if the prostate is irritated PSA may be released into the bloodstream.

So I got drained of a tube full of blood in a minor military extraction and waited for the results with only mild concern—I didn't believe I had prostate cancer.

The results came back in a few days and I was surprised to find that indeed, I had higher than normal levels of PSA.

But there are lots of reasons that a prostate might release PSA. First, PSA levels tend to increase naturally as the prostate enlarges with age. Physical trauma can also result in elevated PSA levels. You might see an increase in PSA after an injury or a digital rectal exam. You might see a rise in PSA after sex, especially if you do it right. You might even see an elevated PSA level after riding a bicycle. You would definitely see an increase in PSA levels if you had sex while riding a bicycle.

On the other hand, a high PSA count is also a sign of prostate cancer. So if your PSA is high, pray it is only from an enlarged, inflamed or infected prostate and while you are at it, pray for world peace and good urine flow (in that order).

If your PSA level is high enough, or if it is still relatively low, but has been increasing over time at a high velocity, your physician will probably send you to a Urologist for a biopsy. I thought the DRE was particularly cruel probe. But a finger that goes in and comes out with nothing but a bad memory beats the hell out of the more invasive transrectal ultrasound probe that travels up the bum to extract cell samples from your prostate.

They tell you that a biopsy will not really hurt, and in the strictest sense, that is true. It's more like the unpleasantness of having your teeth cleaned by the hygienist but in this case they are working up your butt. Although I never cried after a teeth cleaning.

The Ultimate Probe: The Biopsy. Club Med finally got one right in naming the biopsy. It sounds so innocent—biopsy. Almost cute—biopsy. Aw, look at the little biopsy—isn't it sweet. Honey, Biopsy made poo in the living room, can you clean it up? Betty Biopsy. It sounds like they're just gonna take a little snip…not a lot, just a little off the top. It sounds innocent but it is worse. They are going to take a little off the bottom—your bottom.

And they do it with this. A transrectal ultrasound probe, or TRUS.

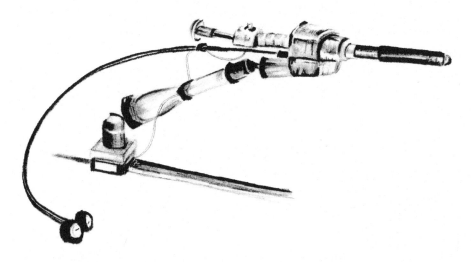

The Urologist's Weapon of Choice: TRUS AK47

Yes, it looks like something we would use in combat. One look at this baby and the insurgency would redeploy to a theater dominated by Eastern medicine. At least acupuncture needles are applied externally. But this? Lock and load, ba-

27

by. Before you freak out, realize that the little tube that sticks out the right side is the only part that enters your butt—not that this makes you feel great—it definitely won't feel great, but at least they don't cram the whole damn thing up there. This baby is a robot guided model—I recommend a hand job—excuse me—the type that is guided manually by the Urologist. There is just something about the human touch.

And so it goes. My PSA was high—the doctor was concerned—he scheduled the biopsy. I was concerned too. But I still didn't think I had prostate cancer.

I showed up, apprehensively, at Dr. (U)rology's office. I was directed to Examining Room 2. You would think that it would all be about No. 1 at a Dr. U's office, but No. 2 comes into play much more than you would think. It's a backdoor approach to a front door problem. I guess if the front door is broken, sometimes you must go through the back door to fix it.

I put on the lovely gown and the urologist positioned me on the examination table in the fetal position. In an act of civility and foreshadowing he applied lubrication where no lubrication should be and gently inserted the TRUS up my bum—he bounced sound waves to get an image of my prostate to help guide the needle. Oh yeah. A biopsy of the prostate involves needles—maybe a dozen pokes—six or so on each side of the prostate so they can drag a sample of cells out for analysis.

I wasn't looking forward to meeting the needle. It's a shard of metal coming at you at a gazillion miles per hour of spring loaded action. Oh, don't worry, after they insert the probe, they numb the area so that the needles feel more like a pinch than the jolting pain of a nail ejected from an air gun into your deepest secret—Victor's Secret. But the moment the TRUS was inserted, I was thinking I needed something stronger than lidocaine—scotch or an opiate would be appropriate.

Now if the doctor detected a suspicious mass during your DRE, the needle can be guided right into that lump in your rump; if there is no area of specific concern, about a dozen samples will be taken—six from each side of the prostate.

What was I thinking and feeling in the few minutes between the first and last needle? What can I compare it to? Waiting for each of the twelve samples to be drawn was much worse than waiting for each well-earned swat of a wooden paddle in my junior high school principal's office. There was nothing I could do to stop it—I just waited for it to be over. Each thrust of the needle was another dead moment passing. It didn't really hurt, but I did cry on the ride home.

Ha.

Dan Laszlo

.

CHAPTER 3

YOU CAN CATCH CANCER OVER THE PHONE

Dr. U told us to call him a few days after the biopsy and Leah and I gathered around the speakerphone in anticipation of good news.

"I'm sorry," Dr. U. said, with a thud. "The biopsy came back positive."

Oh shit, positive is bad; negative is good.

I was getting my biopsy results over the phone. I don't know if that is common. For good news, maybe. But I'm learning I have cancer over the phone? Over the phone!

When I was a kid my mother taught me that nice boys don't even break up with their girlfriend over the phone. And my doctor was telling me I had cancer? Over the phone?

It must be this new generation of doctors.

What's the next generation going to do, text you?

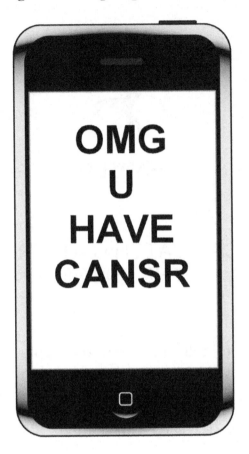

Dr. U. continued. "The good news is that it appears to be a low grade, garden variety cancer and there is a very good chance it is localized," he stated evenly.

These guys must have to give bad news a lot—picture yourself in his shoes. Now, picture yourself in mine—I'm hearing I have cancer over the phone. I didn't expect a house call or a singing telegram. But I sure didn't imagine a phone call.

What the hell is garden variety cancer? Garden variety: adjective. common, usual, or ordinary; unexceptional.

So I had a common cancer, you know, the usual, ordinary kind of cancer. It was unexceptional cancer. I'm grateful that it wasn't an exotic variety, but to be honest, I thought that prostate cancer was prostate cancer. I didn't think that there were "varieties."

But there are. According to prostate cancer researcher Eva Emerson[1], "...the majority of tumors grow very slowly and do not prove fatal. What lends urgency to a diagnosis of prostate cancer is that a small fraction of men do have an aggressive, life-threatening form of prostate cancer. And telling the two kinds apart remains difficult."

Dr. U. spent a little time talking with us—the prognosis is good—prostate cancer is usually very slow growing—the survival rate is high—there are lots of treatments. We made an appointment to get more details and to discuss next steps.

We were numb. And of course I went through some soul searching imagining my family carrying on if I didn't survive. But I'm not going to bore you—that's not funny. You can get depressed on your own—you don't need me for that.

I had a lot to learn about prostate cancer. Hell, I had a lot to learn about my prostate—I really only had a surface level understanding. I thought the prostate was something old men needed to worry about—not me. At 51 I was relatively young—the average age at diagnosis is about 70.

Mother fucker. I had garden variety cancer.

---

[1] Downloaded from usc.edu/hsc/info/pr/ccr/98spring/prostate.html (9.2.2012)

In The Valley of the Jolly, Ho Ho Ho...

...Garden Variety Cancer

Dan Laszlo

CHAPTER 4

THE GLAND AT THE CENTER
OF THE UNIVERSE

A river runs through it. When you think of the prostate, you probably don't think of romance, but you should. The prostate should be heralded as a symbol as romantic as the heart.

Why? Because it represents the river of love—that is what it enables—Sperm River.

During coitus, fluid from the seminal vesicle rushes to an exciting and covert rendezvous with sperm delivered via the vas deferens. They head to the Prostate Motel which provides complementary fluid to complete the love potion. Muscle contractions that accompany orgasm force a high pressure escape through the penis into the vagina. The sperm continue their journey upstream like salmon on a frenetic race to the spawning grounds, where Ova awaits her one true love.

It happens there—in the prostate———the source of the River of Love.

The heart is a romantic, but overused symbol—from Valentines Day to the doodling of lovesick teenage girls. If the heart symbolizes the spiritual nature of true love then the prostate represents its physical incarnation. The heart creates the will and the prostate creates the way. Trust me, without the prostate, there is no way.

The prostate is the source of the river of love that delivered the seeds of your children. So reserve the heart for Valentines Day. Mothers Day deserves prostate shaped balloons and prostate shaped chocolates. Do you hear me Hallmark?

Mr. Prostate's Neighborhood. The prostate is a gland about the size and shape of a walnut; it sits in front of the rectum and is below the bladder. Its main function is to store and secrete a clear fluid that is one component of semen and it contains muscles that help expel semen during ejaculation. In fact, the prostate is made up of thousands of tiny fluid-producing glands.

Four fun facts. First, the urethra, which is the tube that passes urine out of your body, extends from the bladder, through the prostate, and out the penis. You might guess that the prostate has a lot to do with urinating—and it does. Two primary sphincters control the flow of urine and they happen to be at the top and bottom of the prostate. If you treat the prostate—surgically remove or radiate—it is highly likely that some damage to the urinary sphincters will occur.

Be aware that if you mess with the prostate, you just might piss it off. Piss it off and you just might become an incompetent incontinent. It happened to me.

Second, the prostate is adjacent to the rectum. Each treatment option has its disadvantages—friendly fire from a raygun might just cause collateral damage.

If you mess with the prostate its next door neighbor might get irritated and beat the crap out of you. I have a friend who said it nearly wrecked'm.

Third, the prostate manufactures some of the seminal fluid and its contractions help expel semen during ejaculation. It really is the Love Motel. Note the proximity of the seminal vesicle to the prostate.

Now sing it with me!

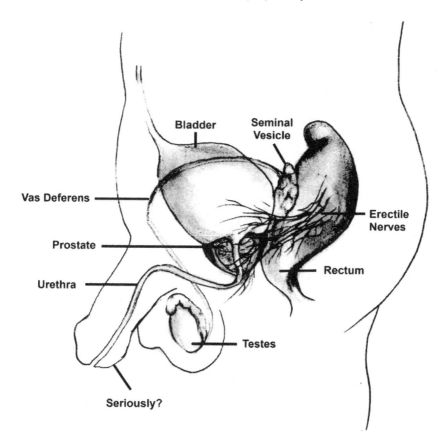

The testes are connected to the vas deferens. The vas deferens is connected to the seminal vesicle. The seminal vesicle is connected to the prostate. The prostate is connected to the urethra. The urethra passes through the penis. And that's where is all comes out.

As the prostate goes, so goes the seminal fluid assembly plant. So mess with the prostate and you just might find yourself high and dry——no seminal fluid. That's right—immaculate ejaculate.

Fourth, the erectile nerves traverse the prostate on their way to the penis. If you treat the prostate—remove or radiate—it is inevitable that some damage to the erectile nerves will occur. Trust me, you don't want to do that unless death is on the line, and maybe not even then. You might just find that you have a lot in common with a lousy actor—you are both unable to perform well. Even if you can get it up, you probably won't keep it up.

In other words, mess with the prostate and you might end up with an erection that fails to show up for inspection. And your vas deferens might just become the vast indifference.

One, two, three, four—now you know why the prostate is the gland at the center of the universe—it is the intersection of coming and going—of sexual, urinary, and bowel functioning. It is central to a hard erection, a powerful ejaculation, a nice long pee and a good poop. Oh, yes, manhood and the prostate are integrally connected.

Erection—ejaculation—peeing—pooping. You know that these functions are central to your manhood. If you can't get it up and keep it up you might as well give it up. A pissing contest determines the alpha male—the winner is the guy who pisses like a racehorse.

The gland at the center of the universe? OK, maybe that is an exaggeration. The gland at the center of manhood?

Dead on.

CHAPTER 5

MY PENIS IS NOT ON MY SIDE. WHY ARE THERE SIDE EFFECTS ON MY PENIS?

Leah and I learned a lot from our visit with Dr. U. I'm going to share some of it with you, enhanced by a bit of spin, fantasy, science fiction and knowledge I gained later.

First, I received good news on the probable state of my cancer. The biopsy sample is typically graded using a scoring system developed by Dr. Donald Gleason in 1974. The Gleason score and your PSA level are used to estimate of the probable stage of the cancer. The best you can hope for is Stage I, which appeared to be my case.

The stages of prostate cancer range from I to IV. In Stage I the cancer is localized—confined to the prostate—and undetectable by touch in a DRE or by imaging technology (maybe the Iphone 6 will have an app that can detect Stage I).

By Stage IV the cancer has metastasized—spread to the lymph nodes or other parts of the body.

If you get a bad grade on your biopsy, indicating a more advanced disease, then additional tests may be conducted to determine the extent of the cancer. It isn't funny if you face higher stages of prostate cancer and I'm sorry if you face this situation.

Those with a garden variety of prostate cancer (now they have me saying it) have to weigh many factors to formulate a plan of action—from your age to the cancer's stage. Your choices include doing nothing (watchful waiting), surgery to remove the prostate, various methods of directing radiation to kill the cancer, some relatively new, less common approaches, and perhaps chemotherapy for more advanced cancer.

This chapter describes the most common options—watchful waiting, radiation therapy, and surgery—radical prostatectomy—and their side effects.

Watchful Waiting

Treatment. The garden variety of prostate cancer is very slow growing. So slow that older patients will probably die of something else—natural causes or heart disease, for example—even if they take no action. You might just live with the cancer and die with the cancer but not die *of* the cancer. Your doctor may recommend *watchful waiting*, which means that your treatment is to be vigilant about actively monitoring your condition so that you are confidence that the cancer remains contained. Watchful waiting is also referred to as expectant management and active surveillance.

I'm thinking that watchful waiting might be hard to explain to my wife or Joe the Bartender at my favorite tavern.

Joe the Bartender: *"What? You got prostate cancer? That sucks man. What'cha gonna do about it?"*

Danny: *"I'm going to watch it, Joe."*

Joe: *"You're gonna watch it? Damn, that's all?"*

Danny: *"No, of course not. I'm also going to wait."*

Joe: *"Wait for what?"*

Danny: *"To die of something else, I guess."*

Watchful waiting? Do nothing about the cancer? It seems hard to believe. But watchful waiting may be the best choice if you are old enough—if you have some other condition that is life threatening—or if the cancer appears to be of small size with a low PSA and a low Gleason score.

Watchful waiting is like a reverse race between doctors—your urologist wants your *other* doctor to guide you to the ultimate finish line first. What the hell is your doctor thinking?

"So, you have heart disease too and your cardiologist is Dr. Lumpkin?"

"Hmmm…Dr. Lumpkin is a terrible doctor. There's no way my patient will die of prostate cancer before that inept son-of-a-bitch kills him off."

"You know," he continues, "Let's not get too aggressive about treating your prostate cancer, right now. I think you'll be dying of something else, my friend."

"What?" you shout in disbelief! "I just found out I have cancer and now you are telling me I have something worse that will kill me first? What? What else do I have? Tell me!"

"Well, I don't really know, you see…"

"You mean I have some rare, unheard of disease?"

"No," he replies, "I just don't think you are in any immediate danger; this cancer is very slow growing. There's no immediate danger. Let's just keep a close eye on it."

But his last question lingers on your mind: "Would you mind paying your bill before you leave?" That is, it is possible to win a race that you are expected to lose.

Who the hell named that treatment? Here is another case where Club Med has done a terrible job of marketing. They have no idea how important branding is. A treatment's name should either be meaningful or mysterious. Tell me exactly what it is—Radiation Therapy—I can understand that—or bedazzle me with scientific prowess—Brachytherapy—I can respect that.

But watchful waiting? Expectant Management? Active Surveillance? Bullshit. Active surveillance sounds like they have James Bond on the job. And I don't know what the hell they mean by expectant management.

And watchful waiting? If you were only watching and waiting I would be all for it. But in reality, if you go this route you are likely to undergo frequent PSA tests and digital rectal exams—like every three to six months. Oh, you thought you were going to get off easy? No radiation. No surgery. But it isn't just watching and waiting. It's probing and poking. Then waiting. Then more probing, poking, and waiting, and on and on until you are dead. Sheesh. So call it what it is.

Bottoms Up

You may feel that watchful waiting is a gamble.. But if your urologist recommends it, he will probably be right. Someday, hopefully many years from now, after you die of something unrelated to p-cancer, your friends will easily identify your urologist at your funeral. He will be the one with the knowing smile on his face telling everyone "I told him so!"

Side Effects of Watchful Waiting. There are no side effects from watchful waiting, uh, unless you consider growing cancer in your prostate a side effect. Remember, this is not a symbiotic relationship—that thing is a parasite. You are not raising a pet. Don't give that tumor a nickname.

True, your prostate is providing a nurturing environment, but rather than being a pet owner, think of yourself as a prison warden. That cancer is sentenced to life within the capsule of the prostate. And this is not some cushy white-collar low security prison—this is Alcatraz.

Be tough, warden; your mercy ended at sentencing cancer to life in prison rather than a death sentence.

Radical Prostatectomy

Treatment. Remember that the urethra runs from the bladder through the prostate and out the penis. Normally, this is just a nice smooth run—piss like a racehorse smooth. Except when you've got a problem with your prostate.

Visualize a water hose (urethra) with a knot somewhere between the faucet (bladder) and the nozzle (penis). The knot limits the water to a trickle. You have to get rid of the knot to water the flowers. A radical prostatectomy is like cutting out the knot (prostate) and splicing the two pieces of hose together. Of course now the hose is a little bit shorter. And when you're trying to water the petunias at the far corner of your wife's garden every inch counts.

If you have a relatively low grade prostate cancer (e.g., localized) you may be a candidate for nerve preserving radical prostatectomy. That's right baby, we're talking about preserving the erectile nerves! Of course, surgery to remove the prostate, splice the urethra, and leave you with your manhood is more complicated than splicing a hose.

It's hard to believe, but before 1980, no one knew where the erectile nerves were located. Imagine, the Viking Landers were sending data to Earth from Mars while the best surgeon on earth was cutting through some poor schmuck's erectile nerves as they removed his prostate. Back then the patient knew he would lose much more than his prostate. Talk about the unkindest cut of all—prior to the 1980s it was virtually guaranteed that the removal of the prostate would leave you living flaccidly ever after.

Then, a miracle seemed to occur. In 1977 a patient of Dr. Patrick Walsh, Professor of Urology at Johns Hopkins University, underwent a radical prostatectomy and later reported full potency. Dr. Walsh took this as a clue rather than a miracle, though I'm sure the patient found religion—I know I would have.

If I anticipated impotence but found the second coming in my own pants—that it had risen—I'd have jumped up and down on Oprah's couch thanking God, Moses, Jesus, Mohammed, Buddha, Pan, Cupid, and Aphrodite! Oh, and I'd thank my wife—my erection would not be complete without her. OK, maybe I would leave Buddha out—Buddha advocates attaining a state of no desire, and if I came through that ED-guarantee with a boner I would take that as a sign—baby, I was meant to lust and fulfill my desires!

Dr. Walsh knew that there was something going on that he did not understand. On February 13, 1981 he solved the mystery. Just in time for Valentines Day! Dr. Walsh and Dr. Peter Donker, a retired professor at Leiden University, were examining a cadaver and discovered that the erectile nerves hugged, but were not embedded in, the prostate.

Dr. Walsh proposed and tested a nerve preserving surgical approach and son-of-a-bitch, it worked! Dr. Walsh is responsible for more erections than Playboy magazine. That's why I call him the "Patron Saint of Erectile Functioning."

Walsh's

Over 1,000,000 Erections Preserved

He should have a sign in his office displaying the current number of erections he has enabled—fewer than the number of hamburgers served by McDonalds but enough to be proud of. Would you like fries with that erection?

You can choose to have a surgeon work by hand or by controlling a robot that wields the scalpel. Patients undergoing robotic surgery tend to lose less blood, spend fewer days with a catheter, recover quicker, and have less scarring.

It takes a surgeon trained and skilled on RoboDoc to do the job well—I wouldn't let a doctor with wet ink on his license slice me up!

But hey, someone has to be first.

Why not you, right?

Wrong. That's what cadavers are for—those stiffs don't have to worry about losing their erections—once rigor mortis sets in they have an eternal stiffy. So find a seasoned pro to work on you. Research indicates that patients of experienced surgeons have lower rates of prostate cancer recurrence than patients of less experienced surgeons[2].

Side Effects of Radical Prostatectomy. Preserving the nerves doesn't mean there won't be damage—you are not likely to wake up from surgery with an erection, no matter how cute your nurse is. You will wake up with a catheter, because you will be in no condition to control your urine for a while.

The ins and outs of incontinence and erectile dysfunction are discussed in detail in Chapters 8 and 9. For now, remember that the prostate is the center of manhood. The urethra runs through it and the erectile nerves surround it. Incontinence and erectile dysfunction await you. How long you will suffer from these conditions depends on your unique situation—it can take years to get all your functions back and some may never fully recover. But doctor, will I ever play the piano again?

Erectile Dysfunction. Leah says sex is all in the brain. And that might be true for her—she will tell you that I'm no expert on the female anatomy or psyche. But it is definitely not true for me and many other men. There is an erection control network connecting the brain to the penis and it includes the erectile nerves that traverse the prostate. Maintaining the health of this network is essential to a natural erection.

[2] Vickers, A.J., Bianco, F.J, Serio, A.M., Eastham, J.A., Schrag, D., Klein, E.A., Reuther, A.M., Kattan, M.W., Pontes, J.E., Scardino, P.T. (2007). The Surgical Learning Curve for Prostate Cancer Control After Radical Prostatectomy. Downloaded from jnci.oxfordjournals.org/content/99/15/1171.full (9.2.2012)

If your doctor believes your cancer has spread to tissue surrounding the prostate then your erectile nerves are likely to be removed. In this case, I'm sorry, but even Viagra will not help you regain your superpowers. But don't lose hope. A penile pump is a great option—most users report a high level of satisfaction with the results. And hey, if it comes with a remote control you can finally stop fighting with your wife over the television remote. She won't need cable's On Demand programming when you offer your own on demand entertainment. And there's beauty in simplicity. Two buttons. Up and Down.

Even if you have nerve preserving surgery, the nerves will probably be damaged. The good news is that you have to regularly exercise those nerves in order to strengthen and repair them. Imagine having doctor's orders to have sex. And for you unattached guys, the associated costs may be covered by your insurance.

53

Incontinence. When it rains it pours. Also when it doesn't rain. The challenge of incontinence is hard to fully comprehend—after we acquire control of our urine we take that gift for granted. If you want a taste of my reality, walk into a crowded drug store, select something nice in adult in-continence-wear, go home and try it on. Not bad. Comfy.

Now, just for fun, pee in it. C'mon, let it out fella! Trust me, it is worse when you have no choice.

If you actually just peed in your diaper, stop reading this book and ask your wife, significant other, partner, or a random stranger to kick you hard in the ass. Then get back to reading this book—you need my help.

Fortunately, most men regain control in stages. At first, if you are like me, you will have to wear Depends—adult diapers—for a while. This is not as humiliating as walking around in a Speedo, but nearly so.

In a few weeks you might remain dry through the night but you will still probably water the family jewels during the day. It is easier to maintain control while you are lying down. Later, you may graduate from diapers to pads—yeah, pads like women use during their periods. But these pads come in blue instead of pink—that'll make you feel better. With luck and time you will soon need just a pad a day.

You may wonder if you will ever be normal again and some men never fully recover. But with time and exercise you may only suffer from stress incontinence—a strong squirt when you laugh, cough, sneeze, or pick up something heavy, like your state of mind.

Some men regain complete control. OK, we know a man can never have complete control of his penis—it acts with a mind of its own—usually an adolescent mind. And after surgery it behaves like an untrained dog—not yet housebroken—just broken. But if you work at it you find your way back—you will deliver urine on demand at least as well as the average 4 year old.

Immaculate Ejaculate. God has a dry sense of humor. Two words—dry orgasm. What the hell? That's right—dry. Remember, seminal fluid is manufactured in the prostate. When the prostate goes you don't come. Nada. Immaculate ejaculate. You can still have an orgasm, but not a sperm will be sprung.

Those peckers are pissing me off.

You might give your wife a radical prostatectomy for her anniversary present—a pearl necklace is nice but my wife says there is nothing like a dry orgasm. All of the fun and none of the mess.

Now, your wife or partner might be pleased, but is there an upside for you? Well, it's a stretch, but now you can fake it. Fake having an orgasm.? Nope. Faking an orgasm might be convenient on occasion. But now you can fake *not having an orgasm*! That's right! There is no evidence!

"Did you come, baby?" your sweetheart asks, breathing hard, after a little moan inadvertently escapes your lips.

"No, baby bad girl," you fib, carefully controlling your breath, "Don't stop!"

Leah says that semen is proof that God is a man. The Divine Feminine would have embedded sperm in strings of diamonds and pearls ejaculated in delight. Once the package was delivered, instead of asking for a warm wet washcloth, your grateful partner would be standing over her jewelry box. Imagine the sensual sight of diamonds, rubies, and pearls free falling from her Yoni! "Do me! Do me! Do me!" she'll beckon. Keep extra batteries around for that remote control.

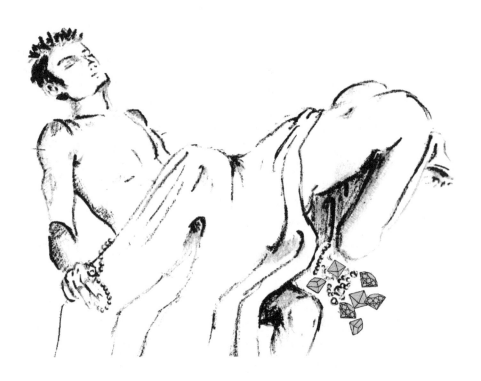

Spit or swallow is an obvious choice.

But before you worry about delivering diamonds you had better focus on the family jewels. A skilled surgeon might preserve your erectile nerves, but most likely they will be damaged.

So, be prepared to be limp for a bit; placidly flaccid if you will. As with incontinence, your functionality will likely return in stages, inch by inch, and it may take years. It took me about four to really hit my stride. For some, it never fully recovers without assistance, but there are lots of fun alternatives to an organic erection. How do you love she? Let me count the ways—Viagra-Cialis-Levitra—penile implants—penis pumps—erection-friendly drugs injected into the penis—your tongue—pages 21-69 of most adult sex toy catalogues.

For better or worse; but mostly for an orgasm. Is a dry orgasm still an orgasm? A dry orgasm sounds like no orgasm to me. How do you disentangle the come from the coming? Do you still say *I'm coming* when no come comes?

Or would it be like a deaf man watching fireworks? They say that losing one sense heightens the others—no sound but bolder colors. What would I gain when my come went? A better fuck face?

I can understand how I would enjoy fireworks without sound but how would I experience an orgasm with no ejaculate? I never thought about deconstructing the orgasm. What are the components that make up the greatest motivator in the world? Motivator? Hell yes, men are motivated by the orgasm. Women should distribute orgasms like kibbles during dog training. They would never have to ask a man to take out the garbage. Just fuck me immediately after I take it out—ok, fuck me after I wash my hands.

Men will do just about anything for an orgasm. And they'll do it often—how frequently do men think about sex—once every eight seconds? And if we don't get an orgasm from positive behaviors, like doing the dishes, we resort to less virtuous behaviors.

The promise of an orgasm impels an otherwise honest man to lie through his teeth about his job—his income—where he lives—who he knows—his marital status—how he feels about kids—his age—his commitment to commitment.

The promise of multiple orgasms is enough for a tightwad to invest in a sports car. The promise of an orgasm can make a man obsess on a woman he will soon abandon in disgust— and the line between obsession and disgust is drawn by a single orgasm. And because a sure guarantee of a plentiful supply of orgasms is a fat wallet, many men spend the best part of their lives toiling in jobs they hate for money they spend on orgasms.

What is an orgasm, anyway? Sex researcher Dr. Alfred Kinsey said that an orgasm "can be likened to the crescendo, climax, and sudden stillness achieved by an orchestra of human emotions." Who can express it better than that?

Of course, that is an elegant description of an orgasm that is shared with your one true love. But for those of you orgasming for sport it is more like that final rush you get on a rollercoaster after enjoying its twists and turns and facial contortions from fighting gravity—when you reach that final plateau—the point of no return—that ecstatic freefall that is pure experience—you forget you—you are just—coming.

Research indicates that male and female brains demonstrate similar changes during orgasm. Brain scans show a temporary reduction in the activity of large parts of the cerebral cortex. This isn't surprising. Men get into bed by thinking with their dicks and women are guided more by their emotions. Why should the brain kick in after we orgasm?

What is an orgasm? First are the involuntary muscle contractions and the associated fuck faces. Second, is the experience of intense pleasure. Third is the ejaculation of semen. Fourth are the moans, groans and shouting of random dialogue from cheap porn movies. Who's your daddy?

I can tell you from experience that muscle contractions accompany a dry orgasm; so does the fuck face. Intense pleasure is still there, I promise. Dirty talk is part of the game but I don't say I'm coming anymore. So we lose one out of four when they take your prostate—ejaculation. One out of four isn't bad but I'd rather give up the faces or dirty chat.

But does the loss of ejaculation diminish the experience of intense pleasure? Well, yes and no. According to research[3] the orgasmic experience is commonly diminished after prostatectomy *but* it improves with time. My experience is that orgasm *is* occasionally less than it was. But when sex is good it is very, very good and when it is bad it is still pretty good. I've never had a bad orgasm, but I really miss making a mess.

Why men turn on the tv after sex. Post-orgasm is a great time to be alive—a deeply relaxing time. The relaxed sexual satisfaction is attributed to the release of prolactin. After or-

---

3 McCullough, A. R. (2005). Sexual Dysfunction after Radical Prostatectomy. Reviews in Urology 7(Suppl 2): S3–S10.

gasm, you enter a period called the *sexual refractory period*, when it is physiologically impossible for a man to orgasm.

No wonder we feel so relaxed. It's the only time men are released from their compulsive orgasm seeking behavior—that exhausting, never ending obsession that impels men to do anything to get a woman into bed. It's not easy being a man with our never ending genetically programmed quest for sex. Except during the period of sexual refraction.

Eighteen year olds have a refractory period of about fifteen minutes, while those in their 70s take about twenty hours, with the average for all men being about a half-hour. No wonder old men seem so relaxed—twenty hours of freedom from the orgasm-quest per ejaculation. And I thought it was retirement. An eighteen year old would have to orgasm eighty times to achieve the same amount of freedom from sexual compulsion as a seventy year old gets from just a single spasm. Eighty times! That's a lot of orgasms. Thank God for the energy of youth.

One little thing. Oh yeah—some men report a shrinking of the penis after radical prostatectomy. More about this later.

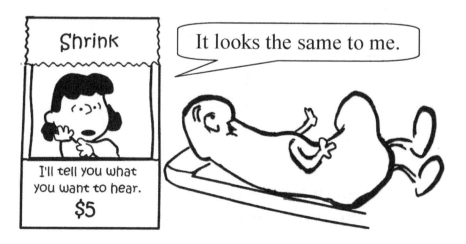

Radiation Therapy

**Every man who was once a boy knows
the side effects of radiation.**

Treatment. There are two categories of radiation therapy used to treat prostate cancer—*Ray Guns* and *Land Mines*.

By Ray Guns I mean external beam radiation therapy and by Land Mines I mean brachytherapy—radioactive seeds that are implanted in the prostate.

Both methods kill cancer by damaging its DNA and ending its ability to reproduce. Cancer reproduces more than Catholics and Orthodox Jews combined, which is quite an achievement since the faithful reproduce by order of God— be fruitful and multiply.

But it is difficult to multiply when your DNA is destroyed.

Ray Guns. The cancer fighting ray gun—external beam radiation therapy, has been around since the 1930's and is continually improving—probably because boys love their toys.

Modern ray guns utilize three-dimensional imaging of the prostate to customize the targeting of the rays. Today's rays are smart bombs that pass through your skin and accurately target the prostate. There is little collateral damage to the skin and healthy organs surrounding the prostate because the rays are precise and not too powerful. Still, some damage may occur over the course of the treatment.

And they are strong enough to damage the cancer's DNA over repeated treatments. Radiation treatments typically occurs over an eight week period for twenty minutes a day, five days a week.

You get weekends off to tan the rest of your body catching rays at the beach.

Take Me to Your Prostate

Over time, ray guns may irritate the skin, leaving a mild sunburn or blisters, but it doesn't leave a tan line. And good news for lovers of Indian food! Researchers have found that curcumin, protects the skin during radiation therapy. Curcumin is a substance contained in turmeric—an essential ingredient of curry.

Turmeric is also in Mulligatawny soup and couscous. So soup, salad and a nice curry should be covered by Blue Cross. The tip is not included—consider it the co-pay.

Land Mines. Planting radioactive land mines—Brachytherapy—involves the stealth placement of radioactive seeds in the prostate when the cancer is sleeping. Unfortunately you will be awake.

When the enemy wakes up, it finds itself in a radioactive mine field—nowhere to run, nowhere to hide—it just has to sit there and take it in the DNA—and then finds itself unable to reproduce.

This is typically an outpatient procedure in which the patient receives local anesthesia and possibly sedation. The metal seeds are about the size of a grain of rice—perfect with a nice curry.

As with the ray gun, there is imaging of the prostate to develop a customized treatment plan to decide how many seeds are necessary and where they are placed. Too few seeds and they may not take out the enemy—too many and they may cause collateral damage.

I don't know whether you glow in the dark after seeds are implanted, but it might come in handy having a glow stick where your penis used to be. Your wife might find that your

aim improves with the aid of a glowing night vision penis—
no more unintended attempts at anal sex—no more wet toilet seats!

The radioactive seeds work a lot like the Neutron Bomb—a weapon investigated decades ago but abandoned by the U.S. Government. Neutron bombs emit radioactive waves so powerful that they kill all life in the target zone but do not affect the physical infrastructure such as buildings or roads. The neutron bomb was abandoned as inhumane, but I have no such qualms about neutron bombing the hell out of prostate cancer—leaving the infrastructure, such as the rectum and urethra, fully intact.

Side Effects of Radiation Therapy. There are side effects for both types of radiation treatments, described next.

Will no procedure respect the measure of a man?. Get this—as with radical prostatectomy, some patients treated with radiation therapy report a decrease in the size of their penises. Men are used to shrinkage, but not this kind. Damn science fiction—the incredible shrinking penis—may not be fiction! We will fully confront el shrinko peno in Chapter 9.

Erectile dysfunction and incontinence. Both types of radiation therapy—ray guns and land mines—can result in frequent urges to urinate and episodes of incontinence. The feelings of urgency may diminish just as erectile dysfunction creeps up on you. What a sad way to achieve balance—just as you are comfortable going again, coming becomes a problem.

Erectile dysfunction may incrementally develop over a year or more—collateral damage of radiation passing through the erectile nerves or damaging blood vessels. Fortunately, nerves can grow back and erectile function tends to improve over time.

You can't win.

Whether you go with surgery or radiation you have a good chance of erectile dysfunction. So, choose your poison. With surgery, you hit rock bottom immediately and improve over the next few years. With radiation, you are fully functional at first, but may gradually lose control before improvement.

Wrecked'm Rectum. The rectum is close to the prostate—close enough to be the avenue of choice when your doctor needs to cop a quick prostate feel. Too close when a ray gun is aimed at your prostate and you are trying not to hit anything else—especially your rectum.

Although modern radiation treatment is increasingly precise, collateral damage to neighboring tissue may occur and bowel dysfunction is a possible side effect. Diarrhea, fecal incontinence, and rectal bleeding may develop over time.

Bowel dysfunction almost makes erectile dysfunction sound like fun. How would a single fellow suffering from bowel dysfunction explain that on a first date?

He: "Yes, prostate cancer was a difficult challenge, but it's all behind me now."

She: "You are very lucky that they caught it so early."

He: "Yep."

She: "So it's all over? No problems?"

He: "Well, I do poop when I sneeze or have an orgasm. And I've learned not to fart in bed. Silent but deadly, in some cases, is not just a saying. I've killed a few bed sheets"

She: *"Oh. I have to go now."*

Nuclear fallout. You will emit radioactivity after seeds are implanted in your prostate. So, Grandpa, you can't let the grandkids sit on your lap for a bit after brachytherapy. Find some other way to spend quality time with the munchkins.

Shooting nukes. After brachytherapy it is possible for a seed to become displaced from the prostate and migrate to nearby parts. In fact, seeds can find a way into your ejaculate.

It is highly recommended that you wear a condom if you are lucky enough to have intercourse after being seeded. If you don't want to wear a condom, you are strongly advised to masturbate a few times before intercourse to clear out any foreign debris.

Or, what they hell. Just take the chance of shooting a nuclear bomb into your wife's vagina—she'll have such a healthy glow.

What a miserable situation! Shooting fire from your penis is a symptom of the disease and shooting nuclear bombs from your penis is a side effect of the treatment! What's next, fireworks erupting from your ass when you sneeze?

But there may be an upside to shooting nukes. And it comes at the time you need it most.

You never notice how prevalent sexuality is until you are feeling the sexual side effects from prostate cancer treatment. Sexuality is everywhere—in magazines and billboards. On television shows, commercials, and in the movies. Sexuality is everywhere except in your pants.

You have a heightened awareness of the sexuality around you when you are dealing with sexual dysfunction. The normal bragging you hear from the Testosterone Boys is even more annoying than usual. You know those Bubbas that market their manhood: "Hey, you know what they say about Italian guys—I can't wear condoms, they're just too tight," or "She could barely walk after I was through…"

That's when it's time to pull out the big guns. After Brachy-therapy, blow them away with your powers. Just say…"Big deal, I can launch nuclear bombs from my cock."

Cancer Wars: A New Hope. There are many alternative prostate cancer treatments including cryoablation—freezing the cancer; thermal ablation—burning the cancer; and proton beam therapy—beaming your prostate to the Starship Enterprise for 23rd century treatment.

Proton beam therapists direct high energy protons to the tumor, reportedly with more precision than traditional radiation methods. Advocates claim that it results in fewer side effects.

More advanced cases of prostate cancer may require chemotherapy—the intravenous administration of chemical agents that kill rapidly dividing cells. Cancer cells divide rapidly. Unfortunately so do bone marrow cells, cells in the digestive track, and hair cells—which explains the hair loss.

It is painful, has significant side effects, and is reserved for more extreme cases. There is nothing funny about chemo.

Sex and the Primal Prostate. Prostate cancer treatment is an active area of research and your treatment options are constantly improving. Who knows what researchers will think of next. Maybe a prostate transplant? Gentlemen, would you check that box on your organ donor card? Would you be comfortable with another man's prostate propelling your semen? How about an animal prostate? My father-in-law has a pig's valve in his heart.

Hey, apes have both prostates and seminal vesicles.

No one, to my knowledge is conducting active research in ape-to-human prostate transplants. But what if they were?

Imagine, one day prostate cancer treatment, far from dooming us to impotence, may result in a primal side effect—wild jungle monkey sex.

You Jane, me Cheetah?

Dan Laszlo

CHAPTER 6

THE SPECIALISTS: WEAPONS MASTER VERSUS THE PROSTATE WHISPERER

Dr. U. was even-handed with his recommendations. He set up consults with Dr. R(adiation) and Dr. S(urgery) so I could hear directly from the experts and learn more about my options.

He did not recommend watchful waiting because I was relatively young to be diagnosed with prostate cancer. With so many years ahead of me he thought I would lose the race against prostate cancer before another disease or natural causes would have the chance to take me.

Dr. R., Weapons Master. Dr. R. had a great bedside manner. He was caring, informed, and funny—he was also single and Jewish and Leah spent the first 15 minutes fixated on who she could fix him up with. Oh, yeah, then there was this prostate cancer thing—she started listening—and decided she'd fix him up after he fixed me up.

I didn't expect the recommendation I got from Dr. R. Based on intuition and experience, he suspected that I may have an early phase of an aggressive form of cancer. That was a shock. Hearing the phrase "aggressive form of cancer" was almost as brutal as hearing the C-word in the first place.

A couple of factors made him suspicious. First, at 51, I was young for prostate cancer—the average age of diagnosis is 70. Second, I had prostate cancer despite very low testosterone levels—testosterone is fuel for prostate cancer—so this must be the mother of all prostate cancers to hit someone so young and with such sissy levels of testosterone. He recommended, in his words, *the Rolls Royce of treatments*—I call it the Rambo Approach—bring out the full arsenal and watch lots of bombs explode in and around my prostate. His triple assault included:

1. Hormone therapy for several months to shrink the tumor and isolate the target;

2. Ray Guns! External Beam Radiation therapy 5 days a week for 8 weeks; and

3. Land Mines! Brachytherapy—radioactive seeds to seal the deal.

This was the first I'd heard of hormone therapy to treat prostate cancer. Hormone treatment is also known as androgen-deprivation therapy. The goal is to reduce the level of male hormones, called androgens, in the body to shrink the cancer and make it a compact target for the ray gun.

Androgen Therapy? The term *androgyny* is derived from two Greek words—anér—man, and gyné—woman. They were going to trade my Y-chromosone for another X! Hell, my testosterone level was nearly zero already. This was adding insult to cancer. They were going to transform me into a woman. Women don't have prostates—I would be cured by virtue of my kinder, gentler sex.

The Weapons Master

Well, if hormone therapy was my destiny then I may as well make the most of it—being a woman could have its advantages. I would ply my feminine charms to get the best possible treatment—all's fair in love and cancer! It was time for my inner gal to check out that engaging Dr. R. And wouldn't my mother be proud if she had a doctor for a son-in-law! I wondered if Dr. R's proximity to so many ray guns had any effect on his own functions. I didn't want to rush into this—I'd put Leah on it. Of course, she might be competition after they turn me! She might be after Dr. R for herself! Oooh that bitch!

OK, back to reality—Dr. R(ambo). prescribed shock and awe—hormones, ray guns, and land mines. Better get the curry and marshmallows ready. I seriously considered his recommendation. And then I met Dr. S(urgery).

Dr. S., The Prostate Whisperer. Dr. S. is a local legend among the prostate-challenged. He has an excellent reputation for being able to remove the gland and retain the function.

I was anxious to meet him, but first I was routed to Dr. Psy. Dr. Psy, The Prostate Whisperer's sidekick, is a prostate psychic—if I had prostate cancer he would see it—he had the vision. No one told me that he would use an ultrasound probe as his Ouija board. Here we go again. Dr Psy saw me grimacing as he drove a probe merrily down my lane. He honestly told me that I'd get used to it. Those words didn't comfort me any more than they bring solace to a new prison inmate.

They say good things come in small packages. Unfortunately, this was not the motto of the ultrasound probe manufacturer.

The Prostate Whisperer

Dr. Psy communicated with the spirits on the other side—the other side of my butt. Good news emerged from the darkness—he saw nothing. I was told to trust Dr. Psy—he had the power and he believed that I had a very early stage of prostate cancer—Stage T1—confined to the prostate and not detectable by DRE or ultrasound. Dr. Psy made some notes, patted my butt, and sent me to meet the Prostate Whisperer.

Dr. S. reviewed Dr. Psy's report, my PSA level and my biopsy results. He queried me about my lifestyle and health history. He was a bit puzzled at Dr. R's recommendation of shock and awe and with the kind of confidence you want in the man who would hold your life and prostate in his hands, he asserted, "You are an excellent candidate for nerve preserving robotic prostatectomy."

He made a very convincing case. I was relatively young and the cancer appeared to be at a very early stage. I could just lose the lump and move on. I liked that logic—no prostate ergo no prostate cancer. I especially liked the erectile nerve preserving part.

Decision time: One if by knife. Two if by ray. I learned a lot from the Weapons Master and the Prostate Whisperer. I had information to consider about each treatment, their side effects, and the very nature of my disease.

Dr R., the Weapons Master and his intuition hypothesized an aggressive form of cancer and recommended shock and awe with hormones, ray guns, and land mines.

Dr. S., the Prostate Whisperer and his sidekick Dr. Psy, hypothesized an early stage of cancer and recommended minimally invasive, nerve preserving, radical prostatectomy.

I considered the side effects:

After a prostatectomy I would probably be incontinent and have erectile dysfunction. I might recover most of my urinary functioning relatively quickly but it might take years to achieve partial or full potency. And I might not recover either function completely.

After radiation therapy I would probably become incontinent relatively quickly with erectile dysfunction setting in over time. A steady *decrease* in erectile function was a negative for me. It is a tenet of psychology that expectation strongly affects outcomes—this is known as the *placebo effect*—your body fulfills your expectations. After surgery I would expect to see an increase in sexual function over time—psychology is on my side. But radiation therapy would instill an expectation of a steady decrease in functionality—now psychology works against me. How low could I go?

There was also a matter of convenience. I could spend a few days in the hospital and three or four weeks recovering from surgery or spend a few months with hormone therapy followed by a few months of external beam radiation and then brachytherapy—radioactive seed treatment.

Now, place yourself in my shoes. I had just visited two specialists. I could obtain another opinion, but did I really want one? Would it help or just add a new hypothesis and more confusion to the mix? What if I visited Dr. X and he told me that I should watch it and wait—no hurry—no curry.

I remember thinking, "Damn, I wish it this was less confusing and more clear cut."

Clear cut?

Clear cut?

Clearly cut.

CLEARLY CUT! That was it! That was what I was waiting for! A sign from God—Clearly cut!

Surgery was my heavenly inspired choice. I would follow the voice of my higher power and go with the Prostate Whisperer. That and the following minor influences:

1. Having cancer inside me was abhorrent. I wanted it out of me. Don't write—don't call. Take it or bake it? I say take it.

2. My 7 year old son still climbs into our bed for a snuggle in the morning. Wearing lead underwear to protect him from Brachytherapy's radioactive seeds didn't seem fashionable. Roasting marshmallows over my

radioactive prostate seemed like a great summer activity, but as my feminine side was hormonally enhanced would they go straight to my hips?

3. Surgery would mean a few days in the hospital, two or three weeks to recuperate at home and I'd move on.

   Going Rambo with radiation required a lengthy regime—months of hormones (which would give me time to pick out a few pretty outfits that didn't make my butt look big), months of external beam radiation which would give me time to work on my tan, and an ongoing summer barbecue around my radiated crotch where I would look so fine with my tan and new outfits. Too much for too long.

4. Dr. S. exuded confidence—he had a stellar reputation—and he recommended the erectile nerve preserving procedure.

   He wanted to remove my prostate and replace it with an erectile preserve. This resonated with the aging hippy in me. I would commemorate my prostate by creating a nature preserve—a habitat where wild erections run free.

The Prostate Whisperer was my man! I believed in him and his environmental commitment to preserve erections. I had made my decision.

Dan Laszlo

CHAPTER 7

THE UNKINDEST CUT OF ALL

The highly skilled are in demand—the earliest Dr. S. was available was two full months away. Slow growing or not, the thought of a few months for the cancer to have a chance to escape the prostate scared me. I tried not to visualize those nasty cancer cells, leisurely reproducing, lazily making their way to the edge, or capsule of the prostate, cell by malignant cell, until that critical event when one cell finally breaches the border, ready to reproduce in the lymph nodes or bones.

I pictured the cancer as an inmate in Folsom Prison tunneling patiently for months, maybe for years, with just a rusty spoon, inching its way, day after day, through dirt and rock, around obstructions, until one day, with one final spoonful of dirt, sunlight pokes through, illuminating the cold, dank tunnel. The prisoner's life sentence is over. But if the cancer escapes the prostate your life sentence may have just begun.

So I had a few months to prepare for my robotic, nerve preserving, minimally-invasive radical prostatectomy.

Dr. S. indicated that robotic surgery required your body to be in a somewhat unnatural position, unless you do yoga and have practiced the *downward facing cow at slaughter* stance. Apparently a chain is attached to your ankles and you are hoisted into the air. Then, Rocky Balboa tenderizes your pelvic area with a few low blows before the Robot takes over—lights flash, rotors whirr, and the Robot cries out in alarm.

Danger! Danger! Intruder alert!

My sensors indicate cancer cells are present!

More accurately, once on the operating table, your body is maneuvered so that your head and ass are low and your stomach is high. Dr. S. warned me that this positioning causes physical distress in some patients. If my vital signs indicated an inordinate amount of stress caused by the contortion, he would go to plan B—operate the old fashioned way with a big butcher knife.

P-minus 2 Months. It didn't take a personal trainer to know that a body in good condition is more likely to tolerate the required contortion. I stood in front of the mirror—two hundred seventeen pounds and six feet tall—a body mass index of 29.

I was fat. Yes, fat!

If I had been sipping Jamba Juice instead of inhaling Little Debbie Cream Pies I might have avoided this mess. Diet is associated with prostate cancer—eat more leafy greens and less red meat. Maybe I ate my way to this disease.

Or maybe I didn't masturbate enough. Yep, it turns out that regular masturbation decreases the likelihood of developing prostate cancer[4].

But I had no time to regret steak and whacking off—this was time for action. I exercised and ate well and two months later I weighed 196. I was ready for the robot.

The Night Before. I was required to maintain a liquid diet the night of my last wet orgasm. Poetic justice.

They say you always remember the first time you have sex. I guarantee you will never forget your last full-featured orgasm. I'll always remember the bells and whistles that accompanied love-making that night. Would I ever again hear those moans, those cries of ecstasy, those magic lilting words—"Get me a warm washcloth, honey."

The Flood of Love. January 24, 2008. Five a.m. is a lousy time to have an enema. The other times are lousy too. One might assume that the enema was never the subject of poetry—I thought I might contribute the first such tribute here.

But after a brief search I found the touching poem "The Flood of Love" composed by Joel S. Muttoe in 1867.

---

[4] Downloaded from newscientist.com/article/dn3942-masturbating-may-protect-against-prostate-cancer.html (8.30.2012)

The Flood of Love

Afar down Inkling Way doth exist

A most gregarious specialist

Amidst swallows and daffodils, as you please

Spread fine white wine and selection of cheese.

Withdrawing the veil of laurel thereis found

Trembling flesh, 'ranged in an allured mound.

Young ladies' roly-poly, voluptuous skin

This worldly gentleman doth examine.

The health of ladies he mends when able

By bringing them to an end agreeable.

Inserted in where ordinar'ly they'd seat

Is an upclomb, blossomy treat.

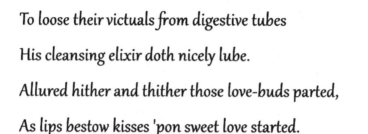

To loose their victuals from digestive tubes

His cleansing elixir doth nicely lube.

Allured hither and thither those love-buds parted,

As lips bestow kisses 'pon sweet love started.

The music it makes is of silent sighs,

Leaving blossomy rains 'gainst sweet young thighs.

From out betwixt that so honeyed cleft

Comes a fierce foamy gush of impressive heft.

Then 'twixt the buds soft silk passes

As he wipes the dew from the satisfied lasses.

Joel S. Muttoe

1828-1909

Lovely. But my self-administered enema was not as erotic as the flood of love presented by the "gregarious specialist." I may have felt differently if a spread of fine white wine and cheese had accompanied the spread of my cheeks. I wasn't thinking—I hadn't prepared a delicious picnic to enjoy with Leah during my enema. I would have, but wine and cheese weren't on my liquid diet and Leah hates to eat alone at an enema.

I don't think a picnic would have enhanced the experience. I can't tell you what I was thinking when I loosed the *fierce foamy gush of impressive heft*, but I certainly did fiercely loose it. And then I did fiercely don loose clothing as requested by the hospital.

Clean inside and out, Leah accompanied my prostate as it walked its last mile. It may have been experiencing more than separation anxiety—this wasn't a farewell party—it was an execution. And no pardon was coming. The fate of my prostate was sealed as I signed papers giving the University of California, San Francisco permission to remove it and display it on a set of lab slides.

A calm fog settled in as I prepared for surgery. I donned a gown and waited quietly with Leah until I was wheeled down the hall to meet my fate, my driver skillfully dodging staff and other patients on foot, in wheelchairs, and in tricked out beds.

But as I rolled into the operating room all hell broke loose. It was like a scene from E.R. except no one yelled "clear!" Staff were scurrying purposefully about the room; directions flew from surgical masks. Bright lights, big equipment.

Robotic Surgical Staff

The surgery itself was boring. I slept through it. I awoke to a haze in the intensive care unit (ICU), which is not the typical landing berth after a prostatectomy—it's like finding yourself upgraded to First Class from economy. My heart rate had dropped below 35 beats per minute during surgery—not quite dead, but moving in that direction, and they wanted to keep a close eye on me. I have a heart condition on top of my prostate problem—I should say on top of my *former* prostate problem. I was rid of that damn gland; and good riddance. Now I had a *lack of a prostate* problem.

A plastic tube extended out of my penis—a catheter is a strange device, similar to a probe but different enough to place it in a class of its own—legal alien status.

A tiny balloon at the end of the plastic tube keeps the catheter fixed inside the bladder. They didn't tell me who blew up the balloon. I'm not sure I wanted to know. Leah tells me it wasn't her.

There were more signs that my body had been invaded—five small incisions around my belly button. It looked like someone had lousy aim—like trying to put a nail in a stud by luck. The incisions were small enough that I might still have a shot at the Sports Illustrated swimsuit edition. Mental note: The five holes were big enough to play the sympathy factor sometime in the future.

You receive so much sympathy when you are diagnosed with cancer. But once cured—buddy get over it. But the scars, ah, the scars. They remain, waiting to be well-played.

After the fog of sedation lifted, I tried to figure out what the heck RoboDoc needed five holes for.

Here's what I came up with:

1. Scalpel

2. Search light (to find lost scalpel)

3. Suction (to retrieve lost scalpel and remove prostate)

4. Needle & thread (to close and hide the evidence)

5. Finger to hold the knot while closing the incisions

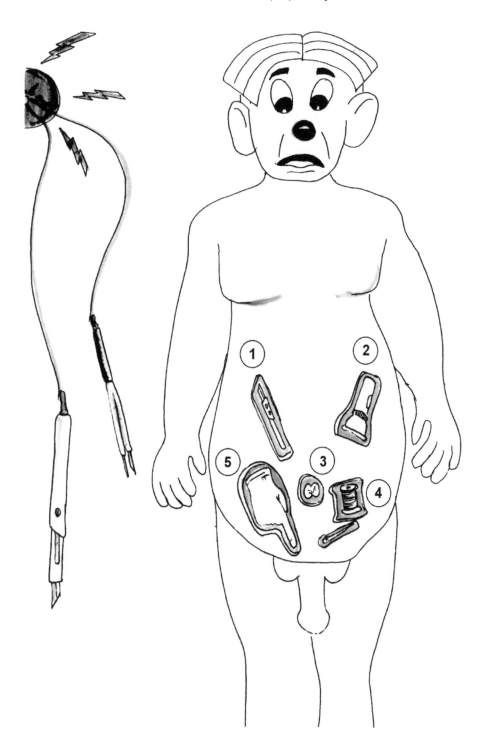

I enjoyed the next few days. How do I spell relief? D-I-L-A-U-D-I-D—a derivative of morphine. I was in absolutely no pain and was in a really good mood. I had tasted the forbidden fruit—Smack—Junk—H—Horse—one could probably make a good living selling this stuff.

They kept me in First Class (ICU) for the remainder of my 3-day all-inclusive stay at Club Med(icated). It is common to be released the day after P-surgery but I guess they figured better safe than dead—malpractice suits are a bitch. My heart problems—a gimpy mitral valve and hypertrophic obstructive cardiomyopathy—may have been interacting with my current battle wounds. My heart rate just wouldn't stay above 35. The monitor kept beeping, as if shouting "This dude is out of here!"

I hadn't anticipated doing calisthenics right after surgery, but there I was in ICU doing leg lifts to bring my heart rate up—anything to quiet the damn monitor. My pre-surgery training regime was finally paying off.

Dr. S. and his posse of prostate pros from Dover stopped in for a look-see. Nothing like hosting a crowd of white-coats for an intimate post-surgical tea party. "It was a textbook case," said Dr. S., "The lymph nodes and surrounding tissue looked good."

Of course, I had to wait for the complete pathology report for an accurate appraisal. Somewhere, a pathologist named Poindexter wearing a standard issue white lab coat was slicing up what used to be *my* prostate. Wafer thin prostate slices would be splayed neatly on glass slides and studied under a microscope. Then I would know the extent of the cancer.

You might think I would pray to a higher power for good news at this point. And I did. But at that moment I had a catheter up my penis, an IV in my arm, and a pillow that needed adjustment. At that moment my higher power was my nurse.

I have always loved nurses—I lived with one once. Nurses have hands that heal. The nursing staff at UCSF was spectacular. And man, they loved to see me fill that catheter bag. "Good for you!" they cooed with real enthusiasm. I guess it is good to know that the hose is connected to the spigot, the obstruction is gone, the splice holds, and the water flows.

But if you really want to bring a smile to your nurse's face, just walk. Nurses love to see patients walk. If you walk farther each day you will have one happy nurse.

If I had known this secret I wouldn't have screwed up my relationship with the nurse in the 1980s. Oh, I peed plenty then too. But I left the toilet seat down. A catheter would have helped our relationship. I walked with her too, but in the end she told me to keep walking. I can still hear her shout "Run, Danny, Run!" as I faded into the sunset. She smiled, realizing that I wasn't getting smaller, I was leaving. I love nurses but they can be fickle.

The next two days were as uneventful as a drugfest in Amsterdam.

In preparation for release, Nurse Jenna emptied my bag one last time. "Good for you!" she said. I'm not as easily impressed. It would take a big boner surrounding that catheter tube to get me to exclaim "Good for you!"

They gave me one last intravenous fix for the ride home until I could fill my prescription for pain meds. They weren't cutting me off cold turkey—they were going to ease me off the Junk with milder opiates—vicodin and oxycodone. With that combination I was going to need rehab. But now I needed hab.

It was good to get home and into my own bed—even if I would have to make it myself and room service was less responsive. Oh, Leah is incredibly supportive, but she believes in tough love: nurture when appropriate but push like Burgess Meredith as Micky—Rocky Balboa's trainer—when discipline was called for.

The catheter bag hung like an albatross around my penis. It would be my constant companion for ten more days. Visitors feel awkward when they see a catheter.

I preferred to think of that bag as a fashion accessory—my European carry-all (pun intended). Fortunately a smaller version was provided for formal wear. It strapped to my leg under my pants—urinating in stealth mode—now that was just creepy. "Hi, how ya doin? I'm peeing."

The Strap-On Catheter:

Have Bag, will Travel

It was time to begin the vacation portion of disability leave—the hard part was over. I was looking forward to *cancer's silver lining*—no email—no voicemail—no work.

I thought I would catch up on a backlog of movies. But first, I was going to settle in and take a nice poop. It had been three days since that dewy enema and I reckoned it was time for a bowel movement—how much crap can a body store before it is permanently impacted? I sat down on my favorite toilet seat, trying to comfortably position the catheter but thirty minutes later I had not purged. Disappointed, I watched a crappy movie.

The Mother of All Bowel Movements. This section is quite graphic, but with God as my witness, it conveys the unenhanced and uncensored truth. I apologize in advance for any trauma you incur in reading it and I pray you never have to sit in my seat. Skip this section if you are a woman or wear sweater vests. This was, without a doubt, the most painful stage of prostate cancer.

Constipation is the anti-probe. No foreign objects are forced into the body; legal residents refuse to leave their crappy little neighborhood. The most common of all gastrointestinal conditions—constipation—is the body's way of telling you that you can't fit a large round peg in a small round hole. Constipation is a common side effect of pain killers and surgery.

Two days and six movies later, still no movement. Our best military minds decided that overwhelming force was our best tactic. We were prepared for the challenge. It was time. I was determined to shit or die trying.

I entered the bathroom with conviction. I had been in firm control for nearly half a century—I wasn't about to start taking crap from my bowels now. My feet were steady as I paced the cold marble floor, surveying the battlefield. The ceramic commode glistened. Somewhere church bells rang twelve times—high noon.

I took this one sitting down. I heard grunts and I heard groans. I heard Godzilla roar. Then, *praise God*, there was a hint of action.

I thought the enemy line had been breached but I was wrong. The pain was searing. The enemy had employed a classic stalling maneuver—I had been outflanked. A burning brick was caught halfway across the enemy line when the truce was declared. It hurt like a son of a bitch. The little shit wouldn't come out and experience told me there was no way in hell it was going back in.

I wasn't a brave soldier. I understand the childbirth thing now, really I do. I started panting—short little puppy dog breaths like I saw in so many movies. Then, loudly breaching the delicate truce I heard a merciful plunk. The battle was over but the little shit won—a short soldier was the enemy's sole casualty.

And our side? We had a broken asshole. Our ground forces humiliated, our military advisors came up with a new tactic-- stool softeners. I won't scar you with further details—war is hell. Weary of battle, I fought the good fight and ultimately prevailed. And I would never forget this pain that I endured in my battle against prostate cancer.

Rehab. I took my pain medication as prescribed but it was gone in five days. I thought the doctor indicated that there would be enough for 10. I called him as I took the last one and he seemed surprised. The instructions indicated a pill every six hours but he insisted the oxycodone should have been taken once every 12 hours.

"I would think that much would make you very lethargic," he stated flatly. Unfortunately, I was too lazy, drowsy, sleepy, soporific, languid, indolent, idle, dull, somnolent, comatose, enervated, debilitated, dispirited, unspirited, torpid, lackluster, sluggish, slothful, indifferent, passive, inert, listless, and apathetic to respond.

I was now off the juice. And when I found myself back in the real world with no more pain killers I found that there was no more pain.

Move. Leah was not as supportive of my commitment to a sedentary recovery as I was. She invented ways for me to help around the house. I was instructed to lift no more than ten pounds of weight for the first few weeks. Consequently, I found Leah with the laundry basket, removing a pair of underwear, then a sock, until a smile lit on her face and the number 10.0 lit the LCD display of the scale beneath it.

I could feel that smile burn a hole in the back of my head all the way to the laundry room. She was determined to see me heal. Very cunning. Of course, this is to be expected from a woman who works tirelessly to convince me that my hobby is construction.

So I moved. I started dressing in street clothes. I walked to the video store. I learned that wearing pants over a catheter is like wearing pants over a stumpy pencil jammed up my cock—a Number One pencil, for a change.

That catheter had to go—the whole damn catheter industry needs to learn the ways of soft silicone. Or the underwear industry needs to produce catheter undies—the catheter tube could pass through a metal grommet on a straight path down the leg instead of taking a hard left or right (how's it hanging?). Maybe boxers are a simpler solution. Now you know.

Praise the Lord, Dr. U. would soon remove the catheter and I would begin my next adventure—Indiana Jones and the Lost Functions: Incontinence and Impotence.

Dan Laszlo

CHAPTER 8

I AM STILL A MAN. A MAN IN A DIAPER

With ten days at home it was time to put space between the tube and my penis. But I had become soft. The thought of having to stand in front of a toilet to pee seemed like too much work now. If they upgraded the hardware, a catheter might have real appeal to a couch potato. And while a perpetually dry toilet seat promoted harmony in the family, the tube had to go.

It was a short visit with Dr. U. A brief update on what to expect—incontinence—and how to treat it—Kegel exercises—was followed by a gentle tug and a very odd and unfamiliar sensation as the tube was snaked out of my penis. I'm glad I was asleep when it was inserted.

The relief was immediate. My penis could move to the left. My penis could move to the right. It just couldn't do the hokey-pokey.

I placed one of my wife's pads in my underwear. Dr. U. warned me that this would not be sufficient—I should stop at the drug store for something more substantial. I had no reason to doubt him—especially since it appeared to be high tide below my waist. I reinforced the pad with some paper towels and prepared to leave—but not before I displayed a bit of optimism:

"Dr. U., Can I try to get an erection?"

"No, not yet. Give it more time to heal," he said.

That made sense to me. No need to start tugging on a urethra that was recently spliced. I wet my pants as I waited for the receptionist to complete the paperwork. My wife's feminine hygiene pad was not man enough for the job.

I was out the door and in a drug store within minutes. I was surrounded by too many choices in an aisle of incontinence-wear. A whole aisle. I would do more intelligent shopping later—in a panic I grabbed a package of enormous diapers and hightailed it to the register as a warm moist blot spread the news—I was incontinent! I maintained my cool. I could do this. I have faced challenges greater than this and I peed my pants then too.

I sped to a nearby restaurant. A diaper was slipped in a newspaper under my arm—I was in stealth mode here. Like an incontinent secret agent, I stole my way to the bathroom. My pants instantly found my ankles. I was soaked.

I examined the diaper. It's shape and sticky tabs were familiar. I had placed my son in a smaller version not so long ago on a changing table in a family-friendly bathroom. But this time, like my therapist tells me, I had to change myself.

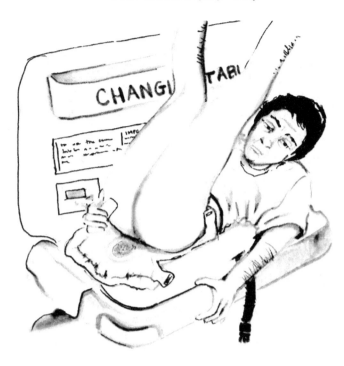

I placed the diaper between my legs. I stretched the back around my rear, placed the front around my crotch and let the sticky tabs find their partner tabs—not a perfect fit but it would do.

I felt ridiculous—I was glad there was no mirror in the stall. Then I pulled up my dignity with my pants. With my urine contained and my self-respect restored I walked out the bathroom door, head held high, minus one pair of underwear lost in the struggle, another victim of prostate cancer.

I was happy to have a finger in the dike, so to speak. I had been unprepared for the flash flood—a feminine hygiene pad is no match for the male bladder. In haste I had made a poor choice of diapers. Go for the adult version of the big-boy pull-on diaper that kids transition to when they are large-ly potty-trained—not the tabbed variety.

I am an incompetent incontinent. The first few days after de-catheterization were depressing. When it rained it poured. It also poured when it was sunny, cloudy, foggy, or when there was weather. I had no idea my bladder would spend urine with no interest in saving for the future. It's 401K was drained. It may as well have been called a pre-urethra, because it certainly was not acting like a bladder. The bladder "holds" urine until you are ready to pass it. There was no holding here—just passing. And passing is the easy part—gravity takes care of that. It is the holding part that is important.

I did not handle incontinence well. I was so fearful of blotting my pants again that I armed myself to the teeth with protection. I wore heavy duty pads *under* a maximum absorbency diaper *under* my underwear *under* my pants. That was some protection under there, let me tell you.

My pants were pretty tight. They were dry, but boy-oh-boy were they tight. Thank god for my fat pants—I knew it was smart to keep them in case I got fat or incontinent. But I didn't leak. I could have pissed the Amazon and stayed dry. This was ridiculous. I was an incompetent incontinent. I am a control freak who was not in control. That just left me being a freak.

Why does prostate cancer cause incontinence? Check out the locations of the internal and external urethral orifices, or sphincters. The internal urethral sphincter is under involuntary control—it's as automatic as your heartbeat—and it is the primary muscle controlling the flow of urine from the bladder. The external urethral orifice is under voluntary control—this sphincter opens on command and is the secondary muscle controlling urine flow. And guess what? There are no other muscles to control urine flow! That's it! The internal and external sphincters.

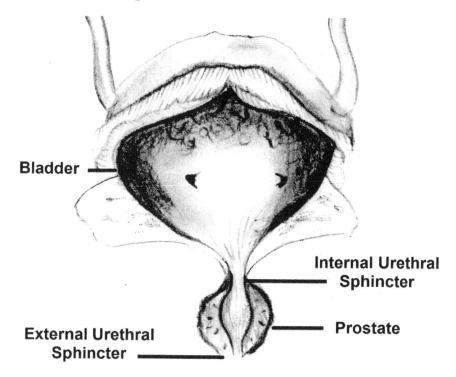

Bladder

Internal Urethral Sphincter

Prostate

External Urethral Sphincter

The Bladder and the Prostate

Two sphincters should be plenty, but take no comfort in numbers. Locate the internal and external sphincters in the figure. Anything jump out at you? Take a good look below the internal and above the external sphincter! That's right Billy Bob, there's a prostate between those two stinking sphincters!

Whose bright idea was it to place our primary and backup piss inhibitors on either side of the prostate? I suppose God thought that the Tree of Knowledge was pretty secure—no need to anticipate radical prostatectomy. God intended us to prance around, fruitful and naked, in the Garden of Eden.

And prostate cancer doesn't grow in the Garden of Eden. Did you learn how to grow a new urethral sphincter when you tasted of the Tree of Knowledge, Eve?

Well, now that you see the physical arrangement of the urinary sphincters, it is not surprising that these babies are damaged when the prostate is removed. Mine were shot. And while there is no third sphincter ready to spring into action, there is a muscle that can be trained to act as a urethral sphincter—the pubococcygeus muscle (pronounced pew-bow-cock-sidge-ee-us). If you maintain your training regime, this single muscle may just be sphincter enough to hold back the waters.

A man in a diaper. I saw Dr. U again two weeks after my catheter was removed. He wasn't happy with my post-surgery PSA test. The PSA level was .7 and should have been less than .2. Dr. U offered three possibilities:

1. The PSA level could be coming down slowly after a successful surgery.

2. Some non-noncancerous prostate tissue may remain.

3. Prostate cancer that was not caught by the surgery might remain.

I wasn't going to worry—we'd try watchful waiting until the next PSA. Then I got optimistic.

"Dr. U., Can I try to get an erection? "

"Yes, you should," he replied. He wrote a prescription for Viagra- and told me to take one every three days and to *do something.* I got the idea. I also got the OK to exercise again.

I found myself in the gym a few days later working to get my mojo back. I was changing my clothes in a crowded locker room, thinking about my workout—it was over a month and a surgery since I last sweated. I was shocked to look down and see myself almost fully undressed—I was naked but for my diaper.

I looked around and no one was staring, but that didn't matter. I felt my face burning and saw myself through their eyes. Then I saw myself through my eyes. I had come through a lot and it came down to this. I fought the urge to hurry my gym shorts on. Instead, I stood there, lingering, daring anyone to stare, and silently proclaimed,

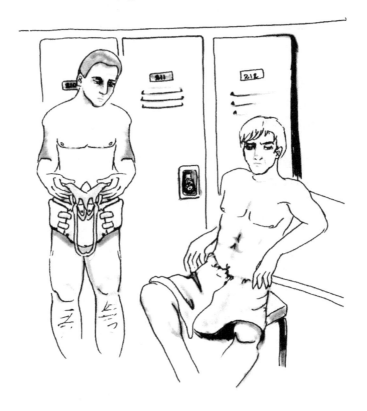

"I am still a man. A man in a diaper!"

I casually put my shorts on, having looked into the mirror, seen my ridiculous image, and laughed with myself. Then I had a great workout. And I squirted a little squirt with each curl and press.

Yeah, my diapers are big. Everything is big in Texas. If you are uncomfortable buying Tampons for your wife or girlfriend you might want to choose watchful waiting over prostatectomy or radiation. Your dignity might not make it through the check-out line with Texas-sized diapers.

But here is a trick to maintain your dignity, cowboy. Scratch out the bar code on a strategic product and wait for the cashier to use the loudspeaker:

> "Yo, Joe—I need a price check on a 12-pack of condoms—Trojan magnums—you know, the big ones!"

Then whistle the theme to Rawhide as you leave, walking tall in your bulging diaper.

Championship Kegeling. Women kegel to tighten their vaginas and treat post-childbirth incontinence. The prostate-free do it to develop a pseudo-urinary sphincter. I hate exercise as much as the next fat American but I also hate peeing in my pants.

Kegel exercises are performed by tensing the pubococcygeus muscle. You already do this when you take those final squirts at the end of a pee and the head of your penis bobs up and down like the most agreeable organ.

Kegel training begins by learning to isolate the pubococcygeus muscle. To begin, go get naked in the bathroom. If your wife or significant likes to humiliate you, she can join in the fun. Now, try to bob your penis without touching it. Next, try to pace your penis to the beat of classic rock. When you have mastered the Rolling Stones you can advance to disco. When you can bounce to the Bee Gees you are ready for strength training, grasshopper.

Attach a ping-pong ball to a string, gently tie it to your penis, and proceed: up—down—up—down. Practice lifting progressively heavier objects. From ping pong to whiffle balls; from whiffle balls to tennis balls, baseballs and the ultimate challenge—the bowling ball. When you can lift the bowling ball with your penis alone you will be cured of incontinence.

Of course this is satire. Do NOT tie anything to your penis except for approved devices purchased from a reputable adult sex shop. And this kegeling is not to be confused with the German bowling game—different balls are involved.

Listen to me. Kegeling is no gimmick. It's not a joke. It's the real deal. Leah showed me a Kegel yoga pose that is an incontinence killer—Downward Bearing Sphincter. If you haven't tried yoga before, don't worry...

It's like
this ↓

not
this ↓

The Stages of Incontinence. I proceeded through the three stages of incontinence relatively quickly.

1. A few days post-catheter and I managed to stay dry at night—the first step toward continence. This put me at the level of the average 6 year old. Good for me!

2. After a week or two I hit the next target—the ability to hold my liquid while carrying out simple, non-stressful, activities. It's good manners to hold your pee while standing around the water-cooler chatting with friends and co-workers.

3. The last hurdle is stress-incontinence. Stress incontinence manifests as a quick squirt in response to a laugh, a cough, or a sneeze. It may occur when lifting something heavy—or from a sharp elbow in the side from your wife. Stress-incontinence can be tough to overcome. More than a few women have confided to me that they carry spare undies in their purses in case a good sneeze gets them.

The Stages of Peeing. There are typically three stages of peeing. In the first stage we are babies in free-pee—no control. Wet the bed and spring forth like a fountain on the changing table; let the changer beware. As young men we enter the second stage in which we piss like racehorses—we can hit a target dead center from six feet away. And when we are young teens we do it competitively. Age takes us into what is often the final stage. Our prostates rebel, our flow eases, and we pee with restricted vigor, if not in drips and dribbles. Sadly, for many this is the last stage.

But if you are fortunate enough to have prostate cancer and undergo radical prostatectomy you may pick up an extra three stages—call them PP1, PP2, and PP3—Post-prostate stages 1, 2, and 3. In PP1 I peed through a catheter tube. In PP2 I free-peed again—incontinence—no control.

But in PP3, shout it from the rooftops, *I peed like a racehorse again!* That's right ladies and gentleman, once the prostate was gone, there was *nothing but urethra*—a straight run from bladder to penis—like a fire hose, baby! In fact, a racehorse can't keep up with me now. A racehorse would feel like a filly; Man O'War might get an inferiority complex peeing next to me.

If I unleash a stream full force, I hurt myself. I can feel the skin nearly peel off the inside of my penis if I bear down. I'm not kidding. I have never tested a full force pee because my penis might explode. Super-streaming is my new super-power. It may be disgusting but it is absolutely true. But like FirePecker, I have a feeling that SuperStreamer will not get his own comic book.

I wonder if I am a freak or if this is typical urinary function-ing after prostatectomy? I'm afraid to find out—if I am a freak the government will lock me up and conduct medical experiments on me in hopes of creating a mutant army. But if I am one of many, then it is time to unite with my fellow SuperStreamers. We will team up like the Justice League or X-Men—but we all have the same power—the power to pee.

SuperStreamers

We are the SuperStreamers, cockfighters united. Our rallying cry? ? We are Number One! Defenders of good, when things are at their worst—when world peace and life as we know it is on the line—the Superstreamers will make the ultimate sacrifice. We will push our flow to the red line and explode our phalli to destroy the enemy.

We will detonate our penises to save the world.

So if you find yourself feeling less of a man in your diaper, you need to walk proudly into the men's room and let your stream do the talking. Just listen to that! The roaring stream screams testosterone.

And that scream is making a statement.

And that statement is…

"Hey man, keep your eyes on your own damn urinal!"

CHAPTER 9

SEX AND THE SINGLE SPHINCTER: THE MYTH OF THE DRY ORGASM

What do you do when you fall off the horse? You get back on.

Shit, that is definitely is not going to work here. Not if I ever expect to have a happy ending to this or any other chapter. Let me begin again.

I love my wife.

And I received a visa from Dr. U. to enter Erection City. Now I just had to, uh, get there. I had to get it up there. Let's get a few things straight here, cowboy. I had a few advantages going into this. First, the average age at diagnosis is 70—and I was 51 and fully functional before surgery.

To be clear, when I say *fully* functional I mean my penis' up and down function worked at appropriate times—I wasn't a circus performer. My other advantage was a supportive wife who thrills me and who was ready, willing, and able (if not anxious) to resume our traditional form of lovemaking. And just to be clear, when I say *traditional*, I mean to add no further details about that.

I mentioned earlier that my testosterone was low and investigating its negative effect on my sex drive led to my diagnosis of prostate cancer. My libido may have diminished but my erecto had not. Before surgery my cock listened to hard rock. Now it was time to assess the damage—did it listen to soft-rock? Or heaven forbid, elevator music?

But first, let me make a confession. I cheated on Dr. U. Even though he warned me not to erectify myself after he removed the catheter, I thought I would just test the waters, maybe just dip a toe. Could I get it to move just a little? What harm could there be in just a little wiggle?

So, two weeks after release from the hospital I toyed with another release. What happened? Let me use a little unappetizing imagery—deboned drumstick. Yep...it just flopped around like small pile of meat with no means of support. To be clear, when I say small I don't mean that small! More like a deboned turkey drumstick. Do Ostrich have drumsticks?

I tried not to overreact to my under-reaction. But this was a strange feeling. A bad feeling. I was impotent. Try saying those words.

"I had cancer."

"I am impotent."

"I am fucked."

I felt like Superman after he lost his powers.

"Up, up, and away!" Nothing but dirt beneath his feet. I imagine he might look around, feeling a bit silly. I mean, you can carry off tights if you can fly. You can wear a cape on your shoulders if you can fly. Superman had a cape and I had the weight of the world. I had lost my powers. And super-streaming was no substitute for an erection.

But that was then. This was now. Superman always gets his powers back, right? I had two thumbs up from Dr. U, two more from my wife, and a little blue pill to boot. I understood the direction. I didn't need a GPS to find *up*. I needed to pray. But praying for a hard cock seemed kind of petty with so many poor people in the world who didn't even have cocks—mostly poor women.

Nonetheless—you pray for peace, you pray for health, but you don't pray for a hard cock. So I prayed for patience. Time was on my side. I didn't expect much. I knew it could take a year or more for the scared turtle to get its mojo back. And women need lots of foreplay. Maybe a year's worth would make up for past performance.

Anyway, Leah was on the bed across the room, wearing only a smile, and yada yada yada...*it moved*!

Not a lot, but it definitely moved. It grew. I know it grew.

That was great news. Like when you think a plant is dead but before you can compost it you notice a little green bud poking out. It's not a healthy plant yet, but you can visualize it fully erect—I mean blooming—in a couple of months.

There would be no intercourse that day, my friend, but the promise was there. Every journey begins with a single step and every erection begins with a semi. Now let me tell you, if you've always had a good erection when you needed one, a limp dick is a sad and strange experience.

I had taken my erection for granted, my friend. Now I know what a miracle of nature an erection is. If I get that super-power back I swear I will never take it for granted again. I will say grace before each erection. Leah will say grace after each erection. And if I do it right, at some point in between she'll converse directly and loudly with God.

The measure of a man. I was doing a bit of research investigating erectile dysfunction when I came across a scientific study[5] measuring penile length following radical prostatectomy.

What the hell? Why were they measuring penile length? Were teenage boys at camp writing research papers?

I read the abstract:

> "Some patients report that the penis is smaller after radical retropubic prostatectomy for prostate cancer."

That got my attention because I had noticed my penis occasionally and uncharacteristically hiding like a scared little turtle since my surgery. There was a scared turtle in my bathtub.

Most men are well aware of the size of their penis. And when you live with your penis long enough (no pun intended) most men come (no pun intended) to accept their size, with a little self-deceit—you may have heard the following joke:

Q: Why are men so good at reading maps?

A: Because men really believe that the following figure is one mile.

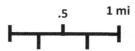

---

[5] Savoie, M., Kim, S. S., & Soloway, M. S. (2003) A prospective study measuring penile length in men treated with radical prostatectomy for prostate cancer. Journal of Urology, 169: 1462-1464.

I continued to read the study:

> "A total of 124 men consented to penile measurements before radical prostatectomy…Repeat measurements were performed at 3-month intervals following surgery. Penile measurements…consisted of flaccid length, stretched length…and circumference."

OK, I had accepted enormous ultrasound equipment aimed at my butt but so help me, keep anyone wielding a ruler away from my flaccid penis. Measuring a flaccid penis is unfair. Everyone knows you measure your penis when you're fully erect. Stretched length? Who was doing the stretching? How hard were they tugging? If I recall correctly, and I do, it hurt when I measured my penis that way as a teenager—especially going for that last quarter inch.

> "The size of the penis was significantly smaller after prostatectomy… Twelve patients (19%) had a 15% or greater decrease in stretched penile length."

The size of the penis was *significantly* smaller after prostatectomy?

That line spoke loudly and carried a small stick. Nineteen percent of the patients in the study had a decrease in stretched penile length.

What is fifteen percent of eight inches? Let's see.

$.15 \times 8 = 1.2$ inches lost.

So *if* I started at eight inches I might end up at 6.8 inches? O.K., that's not bad. But that is a big "if". Now, what's fifteen percent of 6 inches?

.15 x 6 = .9 inches lost.

So if I started at six inches I might end up at 5.1 inches? O.K., that's not good.

Now, let's see. *If* I started at 5 inches...

I finished the article...

> "Conclusions. Our findings support observations of decreased penile length after radical prostatectomy. Men should be counseled before radical prostatectomy that penile shortening may occur."

I agree. Men should be counseled before radical prostatectomy that penile shortening may occur. No one mentioned this to me.

Would it have made a difference?

I knew I might become impotent but I agreed to the surgery.

I knew that I might become incontinent but I agreed to the surgery.

If I knew that I'd lose 15% of my penile length would I have agreed to the surgery? I can only wonder, but it definitely would have given me pause. I'll bet if those researchers had looked a little harder they could have found just one patient whose penis was longer after prostatectomy. Then, patients could be warned that penile shortening or lengthening could occur. You could at least have hope.

Until I read the results of this research study I wasn't aware that penile shrinkage was a possible result of prostate cancer.

Now, I am not obsessed, but I do find myself comparing my current asset to a mental image of its former state.

Making a Mountain out of a Molehill

Not that size really matters, right? It's not like that has ever been an issue! *He's hung like a horse? It's not the meat it's the motion?* If you have to say it's not the meat, then it is the meat. If size doesn't matter we wouldn't have so many phrases to say it doesn't matter.

Picture one of those romance novels with the strapping male on the cover with a nubile female gripping his bare chest. Imagine the following storyline:

> "The Countess's eyes widened at the size of his throbbing manhood."

(So that's what manhood does—it throbs.) The story continues.

> "Her eyes widened and then they squinted. "What happened?" the Countess pleaded. She wore her dismay like a black veil. Her lust died. The throb was only a pulse.

> The mysterious ship captain's eyes sank. "My lady," he confessed, "I did not just return from the lost island of Tortuga as I claimed." His voice broke. "I had a radical prostatectomy," he confessed. "Do you like foreplay?"

The Measuring of a Man. Humans tend to glamorize the past. We remember the good old days through rose colored lenses. But no good can come from false memories that diminish your manhood To save you from this mind fuck, I offer you a "before and after" tool to

> (a) provide an advance indicator of what life might be like with a shorter friend, and

> (b) provide an accurate "before" reference to use when you are staring at your "after" in disbelief.

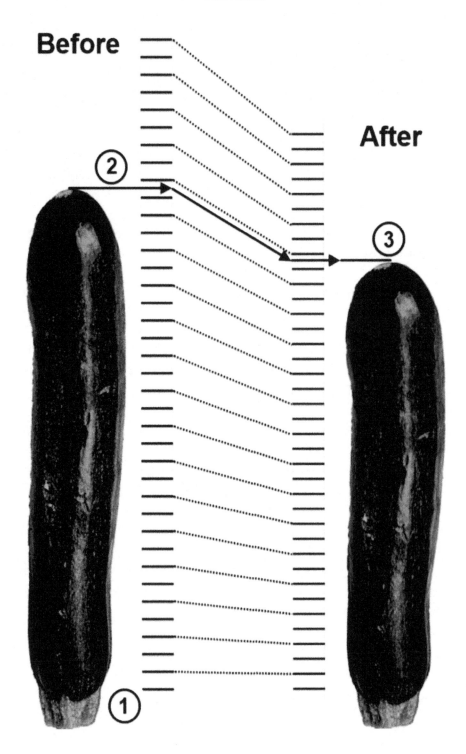

To use this tool:

(1) Place the base of your penis at the bottom of the page in the "Before" column.

(2) Mark the location of the tip of your penis

(3) Follow the lines over to find the associated location in the "After" column. This is an estimate of your post-treatment penis length, assuming a 15% reduction.

(4) Scratch your head and say "What the fuck?"

If your penis is too long to fit on the page then fuck you.

If you bought this book used then use this tool at your own risk.

The Myth of the Dry Orgasm. If you want details on how to have a great sexual relationship after prostate surgery order "The Lovin' Aint Over" by Ralph & Barbara Alterowitz—I'm not about to touch that subject—don't expect intimate details, secret love potions, or suggested positions here. Unless they are really funny. Some people think doggy style is funny. I think camel style is funnier. Camel style is for men troubled with premature ejaculation—camels come in one or two humps.

About 4 months from P-day I dropped a Cialis and a hint to Leah—meet me in bed in an hour, wink, wink. An hour later, I'm elated to be somewhat engorged. Somewhat engorged sounds like more than met the eye. This erection was nothing to brag about, but it was the first time intercourse was possible and we were both pretty stoked about that.

Yada yada yada—it was a love connection and I started to orgasm. *And what the hell?* A miracle occurred! I was ejaculating! I was shocked to feel the sensation of liquid flowing. Then I realized I wasn't coming. *I was going.* I felt urine spewing from my penis like a geyser—and it felt good. I withdrew—peeing in my wife was a bad idea. It turned out that peeing on my wife was also a bad idea, a bad idea whose time had come.

The scene that followed belonged in a Woody Allen film. Our bed was teleported to the center of the Fountains of the Bellagio in Las Vegas. It was wet and wild.

I was horrified and worried that I had no hope for a rematch. But Leah was cool as a cucumber. When the stream receded, my lover, with a wet back, reassured me.

"Dry orgasm, indeed," she smiled, in a dry retort.

God bless Leah. This was a pivotal moment—her reaction would define our sex life for the near future, perhaps for years. It could have sent the turtle permanently into its shell. I could imagine many reactions, but none as cool, loving, or funny as Leah's.

Listen here, my friend. I got lucky. But don't count on luck.

Communicate! Take a dry run with your partner about the possibilities. Dress for the weather.

Prepare! Have lots of dry towels on hand. Stop consuming liquid for four hours prior to sexual activity. Or kegel like hell.

Victoria's Wet and Wild Line

Sex and the Single Sphincter. Remember, the body has two sphincters controlling the urine flow from the bladder—one voluntary and one involuntary—and both are typically damaged during prostate surgery. Kegel exercises enhance the strength of the pubococcygeus muscle and prepare it to function as your single urinary pseudo-sphincter.

I clearly had not done enough kegeling. I had hope that my pseudo-sphincter would eventually have better control during orgasm. But it's hard to control anything during orgasm. If we are lucky, men have a modicum of control up to the moment of orgasm. We remember to put on a condom. We curb our orgasm to please our partner. But once Godzilla is unchained—forget Tokyo—it's gone.

How wrong can an orgasm be? So, you're wondering how my orgasm felt? Anything was possible—men report different orgasmic experiences after prostatectomy. But I think Woody Allen, playing Isaac Davis in his movie classic *Manhattan*, said it best.

> Female Party Guest: I finally had an orgasm, and my doctor told me it was the wrong kind.
>
> Isaac Davis: Did you have the wrong kind? Really? I've never had the wrong kind, ever. My worst one was right on the money.

If ever an orgasm could be the wrong kind, my first post-prostate orgasm should be wrong. It was an orgasm moderated by damaged erectile nerves. It was an orgasm impelled by a diminished erection. It was an orgasm that was supposed to be dry—but urine flowed where semen should.

Yes, if an orgasm could be wrong, that one should have been wrong—but it was not. Not at all. It was very, very right. I'm with Woody on this one—it was right on the money.

Dry orgasm, indeed.

Dan Laszlo

CHAPTER 10

SCIENTIFIC ADVANCES: I HAD PROSTATE CANCER. NOW I HAVE A BIG COCK

Disclaimer: This chapter is a total mind fuck. Unlike the rest of the book, which is humor steeped in reality and fact, this chapter is pure fantasy. Read it with the understanding that I am fucking with your head! If you start thinking "Hey, that sounds like a good idea," then

(a) send me the contents of your checking account and

(b) come back to this paragraph and read the first sentence again.

Pure Fuckery. Medical science constantly advances. Not long ago, well-intended surgeons sliced right through the erectile nerves when removing the prostate, leaving the unfortunate patient permanently impotent. Now, the patient has to be patient, but with time, luck and some fun sex therapy—Bob's your uncle and your boner is back.

Who knows what advances are yet to come? I don't know, but I will tell you my ideas for the next great breakthroughs. Be prepared for uncommon sense and complete malarkey flying in the face of unknown science. I mean, really hold on tight. This may get weird. Indulge me.

I propose that Doctor S, your surgeon, perform three extra mini-procedures while he is in there ripping out your prostate. These three mini-procedures eliminate the three major downers of radical prostatectomy—incontinence, el shrinko peno, and impotence. Let the fuckery begin.

Eliminating Incontinence: The Super-Sphincter. Recall how the internal and external urethral sphincters, which have involuntary and voluntary control of urine flow, respectively, sit at the floor and ceiling of the prostate, illustrated again below.

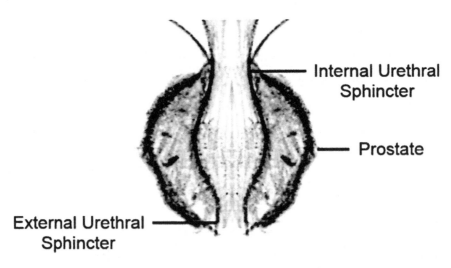

Now, ignoring all facts and way out of touch with reality, I will demonstrate that by precisely mapping the prostate and bladder and by using a really, really, really sharp scalpel and some good stitching the functionality of the internal and external urethral sphincters can be retained, even amplified.

And if a man has both urinary sphincters? Get ready to toss your Depends, boys.

In the following figures I show that with the use of an unsophisticated graphics program like Microsoft Paint, which has been included free in every version of Microsoft Windows since Bill Gates hit puberty, I was able to precisely (1) slice and (2) remove the prostate, (3) bring the fully-preserved sphincters together, and (4) join them to form a super-sphincter.

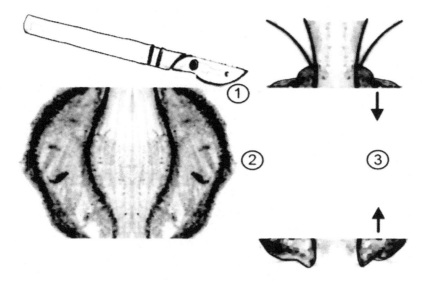

Now, I am not a trained graphic artist. Surely if a complete amateur can do this, then a skilled surgeon can do better with a scalpel.

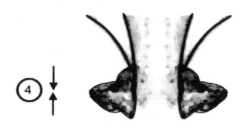

The outcome of fusing the internal and external sphincters is a super-sphincter—the union of the voluntary and involuntary—the conscious and the unconscious. A state of oneness results—one sphincter—a unified urinary system. This is a cosmic cure in continence. A cosmic urine consciousness: Urine cosmic continence.

You're in cosmic consciousness. Young Jedi, you now have full continence and preternatural urine control. The Supersphincter allows you to piss like a racehorse and have a true dry orgasm. If you are into *golden showers,* you might just go with traditional surgery—go with the flow—sing *Old Man River*, old man.

After the prostate is cleanly removed, it makes a very, very nice keychain, illustrated here. See, you didn't lose your prostate. It's still in your pants.

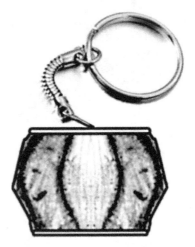

Prostate Keychain

Would you Like to Supersize that Penis? Now that we have cured incontinence let's see if we can help the scared little turtle get its mojo back. The research study that indicated the possibility of a fifteen percent reduction in penis length is not good news for modern man. Size matters. It only doesn't matter when you have a big cock. If you could use a 15% reduction in the size of your penis, then good for you, asshole.

But if you would like to see a 15% *increase* in penis length, read on. According to E. Douglas Whitehead[6], M.D., F.A.C.S. (I'm not making this part up),

> "approximately one-third to one-half of the penis is inside the body, and is internally attached to the undersurface of the pubic bone…Release of [the suspensory] ligament allows the penis to protrude on a straighter path, further outward to give more functional length… This is a relatively minor procedure…I highly recommend use of specially designed penile weights to maximize penile lengthening and combat possible scar formation."

Penile weights?

I was joking when I recommended kegeling with a bowling ball tied to your penis!

So, after Dr. S. removes the prostate and creates the super-sphincter, he can snip the suspensory ligament and allow the penis to reach its full potential.

No more worries of penile shrinkage when you face radical prostatectomy. To the contrary, as they wheel you down the hall to surgery you will find yourself wondering just how much bigger you are going to be.

---

[6] Downloaded from drwhitehead.com/pl.html (8.30.2012)

The authors of the study concluded that men should be counseled that penile shortening may occur as a result of radical prostatectomy. You will still need counseling after radical prostatectomy with penile lengthening—for sensitivity training. You should cover up your enhanced cock when in public showers so you don't make those unfortunate men that still have their prostates feel inadequate.

You can check Dr. Whitehead's website to see some before and after pictures. But be warned—what they eyes have seen cannot be unseen.

Cure for incontinence? Check. Cure for the amazing shrinking penis? Check. We are two for two. Now let's cure impotence.

Dr. Laszlo's Erect Comfort Penis Number. Impotence is a big downer.

Im-po-tent adj.

1. not potent; lacking power or ability.

2. lacking force or effectiveness.

3. unable to attain or sustain a penile erection.

4. sterile.

I have already discussed my experience with my flaccid friend—from the deboned drumstick to driving a semi. This was a mind-fuck no one needs to experience. Why not make the penile implant standard practice during prostatectomy?

According to our friend, E. Douglas Whitehead, M.D., F.A.C.S, "Approximately 30 million men in the United States are impotent." The good doctor describes several types of penile implants that come with different features.

Several types with different features?

What types? Which features? What kind of features do you need except up and down?

Hmmm. Maybe one model comes with a remote control to select your *erect-comfort-penis number*? Why not? You can choose the firmness of your bed so that it is just right—not too hard—not too soft. What a feature! Dr. Laszlo's Erect Comfort Penis Number.

What's your number?

My wife would insist on being in charge of that remote control. Picture this. There you are soundly asleep in the middle of the night when you find yourself rising off the bed! Your wife is smiling at you like the Cheshire Cat—her finger on the "up" button. "I can't sleep," she purrs.

Would she abuse it when she was mad at you? up—down—up—down—up—uP—UP! This could be painful, depending on what you were wearing, or embarrassing, depending on when it was used. Imagine a night out with the boss for a fancy pasta dinner. Your cloth napkin rises from your lap, wiping sauce from your lips while your right hand twirls pasta in a spoon held by your left.

It's not like these implants are unusual or unsafe. And they seem to work. Dr. Whitehead indicates that "(t)he success rate is from 80 to 90% in terms of patient and partner acceptance, and almost 95% in terms of patient satisfaction."

Hell, the implants are FDA approved for God's sake. According to Whitehead approximately 14,000 implants are performed each year.

FDA approved! That makes me feel better—the FDA—the Fucking Device Administration—approves.

Let's face it, a man's potency is vital to his ego. For the love of manhood, make implants standard during prostatectomy!

What harm could come except perhaps a few technical glitches?

For example, with more than two hundred thousand cases of prostate cancer diagnosed a year, chances are that somewhere, two prostate-free studs with the same model of implants live next door to each other—with remotes on the same frequency. What happens when the neighbor's wife decides it's time to play when you're entertaining?

That would be entertaining, but what would you do for a finale? Shoot diamonds from your cock?

Dr. Laszlo's Trifecta. Three for three.

Imagine preparing for surgery expecting preternatural control of your bladder, a bigger penis, a penis that gets as hard as you want on command, and a remote control to boot!

Now imagine coming out of surgery.

You are a bit groggy, but not that groggy.

The first thing you do is lift up your gown to get a gander at Mr. Johnson.

The new and improved Mr. Johnson.

But before you can clear your semi-sedated mind, you feel an odd sensation under the sheet and you hear your wife giggling. And so it goes. You've lost another battle over control of the remote.

The second thing you do is ask how the surgery went. Then you check out Mr. Johnson again. And you think to yourself, what a wonderful world.

And that's the way prostate cancer should be.

Morgasms. According to Wikipedia[7], "Kegels can help men achieve stronger erections and gain greater control over ejaculation…[and] may allow some men to achieve a form of orgasm without allowing ejaculation, and thereby perhaps reach multiple "climaxes" during sexual activity."

Hold the phone! This is not a joke!

The ability to Kegel your way to multiple orgasm is achievable according to Barbara Keesling, Ph.D., author of "How to Make Love all Night (and Drive a Woman Wild): Male Multiple Orgasm and Other Secrets for Prolonged Lovemaking."

Now, I ask you, knowing how men obsess on the orgasm, why the hell aren't there long waiting lists for Kegel classes at the gym? Shouldn't there be Kegel workout infomercials on late night TV?

Picture this infomercial—a spacious room with half a dozen smiling men straining against sleek, chrome plated exercise equipment while perched atop white pedestals arranged in a semi-circle.

Seated at the center of the semi-circle is a smiling celebrity host—maybe Tony Danza. The men bear down on the stylish metal devices, sweating and smiling, while a thumping rock beat drives them on.

---

[7] Downloaded from en.wikipedia.org/wiki/Kegel_exercise (8.9.2008)

The camera zooms in on Tony, who smiles and oozes the following narrative.

"I have two cups of coffee in the morning.

And I enjoy several glasses of wine when I relax in the evening.

Question: Why should I settle for just one orgasm?

Answer: I don't!

Not since I found the Morgasm Pro.

Now, I have as many orgasms as I want or as many as I can bear before I pass out.

And now you can purchase one with just five easy payments.

The Morgasm Pro makes a perfect wedding or divorce present."

The scene transitions to a slick video that shows how the pubococcygeus muscle is isolated and strengthened in only a few minutes a day with the Morgasm Pro. And Dolly Parton makes a guest appearance to close the video.

"Y'all come again real soon!"

I Had Prostate Cancer but Now I Have a Big Cock. Being diagnosed with prostate cancer is traumatic. Life, death, impotence, and incontinence are on the line. So throw us a bone. Make these three modest procedures standard with radical prostatectomy and we who have walked with prostate cancer would strut like John Travolta as Tony Manero in the opening scene of *Saturday Night Fever*—the Bee Gee's thumping disco music driving him down the street with a swagger.

If you don't know him, Tony Manero is a young Italian man who lives in New York City and has the world in his hands.

> "Hey, how you doin' Tony?" a construction worker hammers to his friend with a Bronx accent.

> "I'm doin' great Paulie," Tony shoots back with a big smile, "I had prostate can-suh, but now I got a big cock."

> "No shit Tony? You got prostate can-suh?

> "Prostate can-suh? Fuhget about it! Now I got a big cock wit' a remote!"

Note 1. Remember, this was a farce.

Note 2. The Mayo Clinic does not recommend cutting the suspensory ligament to achieve penile lengthening. They indicate that "cutting the suspensory ligament can cause an erect penis to be unstable and position itself at odd angles, particularly when erect."

Note 3. The penile implant should be considered an irreversible procedure. Removal can cause damage that makes attaining a natural erection unlikely.

CHAPTER 11

BANKRUPTCY

Spoiler Alert: This chapter isn't funny. But it is true. Proceed at your own risk.

Not all cases of prostate cancer have a happy ending. For my partners in prostate cancer who did not, I am grateful for your indulgence. As for me, well, my next and subsequent PSA tests have all been negative—no sign of a problem.

But in reality, it hasn't been all laughs. I understand that I had an aggressive form of prostate cancer and that surgery was the right choice for me. But the intense mind fuck of impotence and the slow road back to manhood was the worst thing I have ever confronted. Worse than the pain of puberty and cruel bullies. Worse than divorce.

Desperately wanting a normal sex life but being unable to perform up to my expectations was my personal bottom. I've had my heart broken by girls I loved but that was nothing compared to being dumped by my manhood. Making up with my manhood took four years; supposedly there is nothing like makeup sex, but in this case, it wasn't as good as the hype.

The first year was the worst. Moving from complete impotence to a semi was encouraging, but I hated taking Viagra and Cialis. The side effects were not terrible, but isn't a headache the most common excuse not to have sex? It is ironic that headaches are a side effect of the cure for sexual dysfunction. Levitra made me nauseous.

My penis, while beginning to respond modestly to physical attention was still an uninvolved stranger. Have you ever talked directly to someone and had them nod as if listening and respond on cue but you could tell they were not present?

That was my penis' reaction to my overtures. It went through the motions of responding a bit but it wasn't there in spirit. My penis had no soul. It is difficult to explain. It was attached to me like my hair was attached to me. My penis grew and my hair grew but I couldn't feel it growing in either case.

I found myself constantly holding my penis when I went to sleep. It felt small—smaller than it used to feel. I'm certain that shrinkage had occurred. I was constantly checking it in disbelief. Was it still smaller? Yep, like an acorn. Are you ready to be friends again? Nope. Depression ensued.

I turned to exotic solutions to impotence. I was determined to save my manhood and for me that meant pleasing my wife. I bought lots of latex and even leather penis rings. I remember rolling four latex rings down to the base of my penis and desperately forcing blood under them into my semi-flaccid penis with some, but little success.

When I attained a semi I found myself in a neurotic rush to get it in and have an orgasm before I lost it. Rather than just trying to please Leah I was all about the penis. I was constantly checking it during sex to see if anything was happening because I couldn't tell without touching it—it was that disconnected from me. And if something was happening it was time to insert it, as if I had to get it to the big sale to redeem my penis coupon before it expired.

Somewhere in that first year I even had the bright idea of buying a strap-on penis. Seriously, I bought one. I thought if I could just please Leah that I would feel better about myself. Leah was mortified. She told me that I just didn't get it. And I knew I didn't get it. But it didn't matter. I wasn't ready to move on or evolve. That was my low. *I was sexually bankrupt.* And even though it was still new in its packaging, that was one unused toy that didn't make it to Goodwill or a garage sale.

Into the second year I lost faith that my penis and I would ever become friends again. My erection was returning— month by month I was able to get a bit harder—sufficient for intercourse—but it still felt like a stranger. I was an outside observer unable to look away from the train wreck. I was lost in limbo. My depression deepened.

Somewhere in the third year I began testosterone therapy. I had let time pass to make sure my PSA levels remained undetectable, and although I was cautioned that there was some risk of the cancer recurring, my quality of life was low and if more energy and muscle mass and a heightened libido would help, I was ready to take the gamble.

I didn't feel much of an effect from the testosterone. I may not have given it a valid trial—I was depressed, less than fully potent, and perhaps not vigilant about the daily application of the testosterone-laden gel. I gave up.

My penis improved—I could get a good erection in the third year but I was still attached to a stranger that peed for me. I was attached to a penis without a personality. It had no heart.

In the science fiction and fantasy movie Avatar, the human protagonist, Jake, and the indigenous species, the Navi, develop deep connections with Ikrans—large dragon-like birds—by connecting their neural braids to those of the fantastic creatures. This is a bond for life and the connection allows the rider to be one with the Ikran—to share its strength and powers when connected. That's how men are connected to their penises. That's how I used to be connected to mine.

In the fourth year I decided to try a more aggressive form of testosterone therapy—injections. Dr. U. ordered another blood test to check my testosterone levels again—it had been years. We had to wait for the results.

On my way out of Dr. U's office, as an afterthought, I mentioned that I had seen a commercial touting Cialis for daily use and asked about it. Cialis for daily use delivers a smaller dosage that builds up in your system over time. The lower dosage is supposed to result in fewer side effects and the regular ingestion is intended to create a perpetual state of erection-readiness. Dr. U. gave me a sample pack and told me to try them.

And my world changed. Over the course of the five days it takes for Cialis daily use to build up, my estranged friend called. It called *me*! "I'm sorry I've been gone so long," Dick said, "I've been traveling abroad. I'm back."

Dick came back. He didn't apologize. We didn't need to talk about it. He was just back and it was if he had never left, like a close friend that just left for a weekend. He isn't quite the same. Something traumatic happened to him while he was away—like he had a minor stroke. But I still love him and for the most part he's the same old Dick.

God bless Eli Lilly. I don't know who Eli or Lilly are, but I'd like to show Eli my gratitude and show Lilly my welcome home Dick. I have no connection with Eli Lilly or Cialis except the emotional one I have developed, so pardon me if this sounds like an infomercial. But Lord help me, I don' t know of a more profound change in my life than that effected by the Big C—Cialis for daily use. When I talk about the Big C now, it is not Cancer I am discussing—I am waxing poetic over Cialis for daily use.

Now the acorn seems like an oak with a real live trunk. I don't have to touch it to believe it—Dick calls *me*—I wake up with erections! It has been four years since I awoke with an erection and now it happens regularly. Regularly! When I pee I have something to hold onto again. My world changed. Superman got his powers back. The scared little turtle found its mojo.

My sex life is improving. Recall that originally it was my reduced libido and not my erection that was the problem. I told Dr. U. about the miracle that had occurred. He told me my testosterone was on the low side of normal, but not outside the normal range, which varies from my original diagnosis. Given Dick's return, he thought that I should reconsider testosterone treatments for now, reintroduce him to Leah, and see what happened.

That's what I am doing and that pretty much leaves me where I was before I found out that I had elevated PSA levels in 2008. Full circle.

I like to say that *all is well that ends*. This challenge is largely behind me. And speaking of behind me, the biggest upside to prostate cancer is not having any damn doctor's finger up my ass for the annual digital rectal exam ever, ever, again. Right?

Wrong. Now in my fifties, I was scheduled for my first colonoscopy. I made it through by flirting with the nurses, of course. "If you happen to find a wedding ring up there..." I joked.

"That's not a joke around here," Laverne said. "You wouldn't believe what we have found up there! Forks. Knifes. A complete set of dentures. Complete! I think someone was having dinner up there," she laughed.

"That's funny," I said. "Hey, that gives me an idea for a book!"

ABOUT THE AUTHOR

Seriously, what more do you want to know?

THE ILLUSTRATOR

Zeana Bey holds a BA in clinical psychology from Richmond University in London. While this has nothing to do with illustration or fine art, it provided her with the emotional and psychological stamina to endure months of drawing and talking about penises and prostates in Starbucks while customers with small children stared in horror. Her current works are on exhibition in a portfolio stashed under her bed.

Made in the USA
Coppell, TX
08 February 2022

73207216R00090